None *but* *the* *brave*

A thought-provoking collection of poems about all kinds of courage – from the soldier's bravery in battle to the different but equally noble courage shown in the face of all kinds of handicap and adversity. The heroes celebrated here are knights of King Arthur's court, a bus conductor with failing kidneys, a group of women who rescue a lifeboat crew, a mother who works all day to earn just two shillings, Second World War pilots, Falklands soldiers, peace women . . . Some poems, as you would expect, are grand, serious, exciting or dramatic, but many more are funny, angry, regretful, or just plain daft.

This is Graeme and Jennifer Curry's second book for Beavers: the first was *The Beaver Book of Revolting Rhymes* – a collection of disgusting verse. Jennifer Curry has also compiled *The Beaver Book of Skool Verse* and *Treasure Trove*.

Also in Beaver Books by Jennifer Curry

The Beaver Book of Skool Verse
Mary Had a Crocodile and other funny animal verse
Treasure Trove
The Beaver Book of Revolting Rhymes
with Graeme Curry

NONE
BUT THE
BRAVE

Compiled by Jennifer and Graeme Curry

Illustrated by David Arthur

Beaver Books

A Beaver Original
Published by Arrow Books Limited
62–65 Chandos Place, London, WC2N 4NW
A division of Century Hutchinson Ltd
London Melbourne Sydney Auckland Johannesburg
and agencies throughout the world

First published in 1986
© Copyright this collection
Jennifer and Graeme Curry 1986
© Copyright illustrations
Century Hutchinson Ltd 1986

Set in Linoterm Bembo
by JH Graphics Limited, Reading, Berks
Printed and bound in Great Britain by
Anchor Brendon Limited, Tiptree, Essex

ISBN 0 09 937360 2

This book is for Lesley's children,
Andrew and Olivia

Introduction

It all began with the war in the Falklands in 1982. The papers and news bulletins were full of stories of death and glory, of our 'brave lads', heroes of the hour and pride of their nation. And then, just as we had finished watching TV coverage of a blood-stained battle at sea, Graeme suddenly said, 'But what *is* brave?'

Silly question. We all know what brave is. It's fighting with courage, refusing to run away or surrender, standing up for our rights, protecting the people and places we love. It's all action-packed, bold and dramatic.

Then we thought of Roger. When Roger was seventeen he was the star of the school rugby team – until he broke his back in the scrum. Now he watches rugby, and life, from his wheelchair. But he's been to university, and he's got himself a good job, and he's always ready with a smile and a joke. That's brave.

And there's Alison who lives round the corner. She's only twelve, but since her mother went away three years ago she's had to take care of her little brothers after school while her father's still at work. She misses her Mum, she's frightened of the dark, and sometimes she's scared of being in charge. But she doesn't complain. She just gets on with it because she knows that her Dad relies on her. That's brave.

And what about pretty, gentle-hearted Mina? Practically every day she is teased and jeered at just because she happens to be born black. But if it makes her cry sometimes she cries alone, when there's no one to see her tears. That's brave.

'None but the brave,' wrote the poet John Dryden, 'deserve the fair.' And none but the brave deserve a place in our book. But whether they are the brave who go adventuring, or who defend our freedom in wars on land, sea and air, or whether they are the brave who wage daily private wars because they are poor or ill or handicapped; afraid or lonely; bullied, tormented or taunted . . . it doesn't matter.

What is brave? Battling on against the odds, having a go, refusing to give in or give up, no matter how hard it is to keep going – *that's* brave.

J.C. & G.C.

Legend

The blacksmith's boy went out with a rifle
and a black dog running behind.
Cobwebs snatched at his feet,
rivers hindered him,
thorn branches caught at his eyes to make him blind
and the sky turned into an unlucky opal,
but he didn't mind.
I can break branches, I can swim rivers, I can stare
    out any spider I meet,
said he to his dog and his rifle.

The blacksmith's boy went over the paddock
with his old black hat on his head.
Mountains jumped in his way,
rocks rolled down on him,
and the old crow cried, You'll soon be dead.
And the rain came down like mattocks.
But he only said
I can climb mountains, I can dodge rocks, I can
    shoot an old crow any day,
and he went on over the paddocks.

When he came to the end of the day the sun began
    falling.
Up came the night ready to swallow him,
like the barrel of a gun,
like an old black hat,
like a black dog hungry to follow him.
Then the pigeon, the magpie and the dove began
    wailing
and the grass lay down to billow him.
His rifle broke, his hat flew away and his dog was
    gone
and the sun was falling.

But in front of the night the rainbow stood on a
    mountain,
just as his heart foretold.
He ran like a hare,
he climbed like a fox;
he caught it in his hands, the colour and the cold—
like a bar of ice, like the column of a fountain,
like a ring of gold.
The pigeon, the magpie and the dove flew up to
    stare,
and the grass stood up again on the mountain.

The blacksmith's boy hung the rainbow on his
    shoulder
instead of his broken gun.
Lizards ran out to see,
snakes made way for him,
and the rainbow shone as brightly as the sun.
All the world said, Nobody is braver, nobody is
    bolder,
nobody else has done
anything to equal it. He went home as bold as he
    could be
with the swinging rainbow on his shoulder.

Judith Wright

The mountaineers

Despite the drums we were ready to go.
The natives warned us shaking their spears.
Soon we'd look down on them a mile below
rather as Icarus, so many poets ago,
waved to those shy, forlorn ones, dumb on a
    thumbnail field.
We started easily but oh the climb was slow.

Above us, the grey perilous rocks like our pride
rose higher and higher – broken teeth of the
    mountain –
while below the dizzy cliffs, the tipsy angles
    signified
breathless vertigo and falling possible suicide.
So we climbed on, roped together. At the night
    camps
our voices babel yet our journey glorified.

The soul too has altitudes and the great birds fly
over. All the summer long we climbed higher,
crag above crag under a copper sulphate sky,
peak above peak singing of the deserted, shy,
inconsolable ones. Still we climb to the chandelier
    stars
and the more we sing the more we die.

So ascending in that high Sinai of the air,
in space and canyons of the spirit, we lost ourselves
amongst the animals of the mountain – the terrible
    stare
of self meeting itself – and no one would dare
return, descend to that most flat and average world.
Rather, we made a small faith out of a tall despair.

Shakespeare, Milton, Wordsworth, came this way
near the lonely precipice, their faces gold
in the marigold sunset. But they could never stay
under the hurricane tree so climbed to allay
that voice which cried: 'You may never climb
    again.'
Our faces too are gold but our feet are clay.

We discovered more than footprints in the snow,
more than mountain ghost, more than desolate
    glory,
yet now, looking down, we see nothing below
except wind, steaming ice, floating mist – and so
silently, sadly, we follow higher the rare songs of
    oxygen.
The more we climb the further we have to go.

                                          Dannie Abse

Mother to son

Well, son, I'll tell you:
Life for me ain't been no crystal stair.
It's had tacks in it,
And splinters,
And boards torn up,
And places with no carpet on the floor—
Bare.
But all the time
I'se been a–climbin' on,
And reachin' landin's,
And turnin' corners,
And sometimes goin' in the dark
Where there ain't been no light.
So, boy, don't you turn back.
Don't you set down on the steps
'Cause you find it kinder hard.
Don't you fall now—
For I'se still goin', honey,
I'se still climbin',
And life for me ain't been no crystal stair.

Langston Hughes

Come another day

Mondays,
my mother chopped wood
and twisted newspaper
to make fire,
beneath a whitened stone
boiler, with a wooden lid
that was itself bleached
white with steam,
to imitate it seemed
an inferno, in which to work
with red hot coals
and scalding water, bubbling,
spitting, foaming, as she
drubbed at sails of linen,
fighting them with a
dolly stick, possessing
all the qualities of driftwood.
Misted in vapour, her hair
was dank and coming
in from school, dinner
was always cold meat
left from Sundays,
with potato mash
wet as the washing.

Mondays,
my mother stood
at the tin bath
and a rubbing board,
with brick hard yellow soap,
battering her knuckles
against zinc, raw
fingers wringing, squeezing
twisting the dirt of life
away, to float as scum
before the operation of
a vast machine of iron cast,
made in Doncaster,
with massive rollers
that mangled buttons
as slowly and certainly
as it mangled my mother.
Home from school,
the end of our day,
we sat upon the floor,
peering under wet clothes
to glimpse the stove,
our comics soggy, as we
munched our bread.

Mondays,
my mother sweated,
heavy black irons
heated on a kitchen range,
gripped with scorching
slipping cloths, to
brand the flesh and
press and hiss the dampness
from the wearying pile,
filling wicker baskets
with sweet smooth warmth,
before she sat by mantle
light, to rummage
in a biscuit tin
matching buttons crushed,
sewing, thin cotton
edges frayed.
From the memory smell
of steam and starch,
childhood skies of Reckitts
blue. I remember,
Mondays, my mother
earned two shillings.

John Gorman

Molly Metcalfe

Old Molly Metcalfe counting sheep
Yan tan tether mether pip she counted
Up upon Swaledale counting sheep
Yan tan tether mether pip she said.

Grow little sheep come hail come snow
Yan tan tether mether pip she counted
Fine warm wool for a gentleman's shoulder blades
Yan tan tether mether pip she said.

Over the heather when the weather is cold
Yan tan tether mether pip she counted
Stiff Molly Metcalfe goes bow leggedly
Yan tan tether mether pip she said.

Grow little sheep come wind come rain
Yan tan tether mether pip she counted
Fine warm wool for a lady's counterpane
Yan tan tether mether pip she said.

On her back in the bracken with frozen bones
Yan tan tether mether pip she counted
Daft Molly Metcalfe singing alone
Yan tan tether mether pip she said.

Grow little sheep come death come dark
Yan tan tether mether pip she counted
No such wool for old Molly Metcalfe
Yan tan tether mether pip she said.

Jake Thackray

The solitary reaper

Behold her, single in the field,
Yon solitary Highland Lass!
Reaping and singing by herself;
Stop here, or gently pass!
Alone she cuts and binds the grain,
And sings a melancholy strain;
O listen! for the vale profound
Is overflowing with the sound.

No nightingale did ever chaunt
More welcome notes to weary bands
Of travellers in some shady haunt,
Among Arabian sands:
A voice so thrilling ne'er was heard
In spring–time from the cuckoo bird.
Breaking the silence of the seas
Among the farthest Hebrides.

Will no one tell me what she sings?
Perhaps the plaintive numbers flow
For old, unhappy, far-off things,
And battles long ago;
Or is it some more humble lay,
Familiar matter of to-day?
Some natural sorrow, loss, or pain,
That has been, and may be again?

Whate'er the theme, the maiden sang
As if her song could have no ending;
I saw her singing at her work,
And o'er the sickle bending—
I listened, motionless and still;
And, as I mounted up the hill,
The music in my heart I bore
Long after it was heard no more.

William Wordsworth

The fiddler

The blind man lifts his violin
And tucks it up right under his chin;
He saws with his fiddle-stick to and fro
And out comes the music sorrowful slow.

Oh Shenandoah, it seems to say,
Good-bye, you rolling river,
To Londonderry I'm away
Beside the weeping willow.

Ha'pennies and pennies he gets but few
As he fiddles his old tunes through and through;
But he nods and smiles as he scrapes away
And out comes the music sprightly and gay.

To the Irish washerwoman dancing a jig
In the land of Sweet Forever
Over the hills goes Tom with his pig,
And it's there we'll surely follow!

James Reeves

Beat that

There's a man who hops at the corner of the street
He hops so fast he's impossible to beat
He hops into town and he hops right out
His hops are so many you can't keep count
He's only one leg and he doesn't use a stick
Jumps like a pogo and lands like a brick

No one's laughed because he's so fast
No one knows his secret for no one dares ask
He'll hop 'til he drop
Or when he want to stop
And he who hops loudest, hops last

Some folks just excel when with a problem faced
Makes me hopping mad for he gives me a taste
Of what it's like to waste
what I got.
I jog a mile or two
It keeps me fit, that's true
But I got two legs
Damnit.

Adrian Mealing

Rufus prays

In the darkening church
 Where but a few had stayed
At the Litany Desk
 The idiot knelt and prayed.

Rufus, stunted, uncouth,
   The one son of his mother.
'Eh, I'd sooner 'ave Rufie,'
   She said, 'than many another:

''E's useful about the 'ouse,
   And so gentle as 'e can be.
An' 'e gets up early o' mornin's
   And makes me a cup o' tea.'

The formal evensong
   Had passed over his head:
He sucked his thumb, and squinted,
   And dreamed, instead.

Now while the organ boomed
   To the few who still were there,
At the Litany Desk
   The idiot made his prayer:

'Gawd bless Mother,
   'N' make Rufie a good lad:
Take Rufie to Heaven
   'N' forgive him when 'e's bad.

'N' early mornin's in Heaven
   'E'll make mother's tea,
'N' a cup for the Lord Jesus
   'N' a cup for Thee.'

L. A. G. Strong

Five years old

Five-year-olds dream of becoming giants—
Golden-bearded, striding around the map,
Gulping streams, munching sandwiches
Of crushed ice and white-hot anthracite
Between two slices of slate.
They sit on the edge of Salisbury Plain
Bawling huge songs across the counties
For ten days at a time,
Eating trees, cuddling carthorses,
Before stomping home to Windsor Castle.
They name clouds. They fall in love with buses,
They lick the stars, they are amazed by hoses,
They dance all the time because they don't think
    about dancing . . .

They long to be allowed into the big good schools
Which will teach them to be giants with wings.

Adrian Mitchell

Haiku

A small sparrow;
Pouting his chest to the world,
He sings his thoughts aloud.

Mark Nathan (11)

A London sparrow's 'If'

If you c'n keep alive when li'l bleeders
   Come arter y' wi' catapults an' stones;
If you c'n grow up unpertickler feeders,
   An' live on rubbidge, crumbs, an' 'addock bones;
If you c'n nest up in the bloomin' gutters,
   An' dodge the blinkin' tabby on the tiles;
Nip under wheels an' never get the flutters,
   Wear brahn an' no bright-coloured fevver-styles;
If you ain't blown b' nippers (Cor, I'd skin 'em!),
   Stop in y'r shells nah, warm-like, under me;
Yours is the eggs an' everyfink 'at's in 'em—
   An' when they 'atch, you be cock-sparrers, see?

J. A. Lindon

from 'If'

If you can keep your head when all about you
    Are losing theirs and blaming it on you;
If you can trust yourself when all men doubt you,
    But make allowance for their doubting too;
If you can wait and not be tired by waiting,
    Or being lied about, don't deal in lies,
Or being hated, don't give way to hating,
    And yet don't look too good, nor talk too wise;

If you can talk with crowds and keep your virtue,
    Or walk with kings – nor lose the common touch;
If neither foes nor loving friends can hurt you;
    If all men count with you, but none too much;
If you can fill the unforgiving minute
    With sixty seconds' worth of distance run,
Yours is the Earth and everything that's in it,
    And – which is more – you'll be a Man, my son!

Rudyard Kipling

The village blacksmith

Under a spreading chestnut-tree
    The village smithy stands;
The smith, a mighty man is he,
    With large and sinewy hands;
And the muscles of his brawny arms
    Are strong as iron bands.

His hair is crisp, and black, and long,
    His face is like the tan;
His brow is wet with honest sweat,
    He earns what'er he can,
And looks the whole world in the face,
    For he owes not any man.

Week in, week out, from morn till night,
    You can hear his bellows blow;
You can hear him swing his heavy sledge,
    With measured beat and slow,
Like a sexton ringing the village bell,
    When the evening sun is low.

And children coming home from school
    Look in at the open door;
They love to see the flaming forge,
    And hear the bellows roar,
And catch the burning sparks that fly
    Like chaff from a threshing-floor.

He goes on Sunday to the church,
    And sits among his boys;
He hears the parson pray and preach,
    He hears his daughter's voice
Singing in the village choir,
    And it makes his heart rejoice.

It sounds to him like her mother's voice,
    Singing in Paradise!
He needs must think of her once more,
    How in the grave she lies;
And with his hard, rough hand he wipes
    A tear out of his eyes.

Toiling – rejoicing – sorrowing,
    Onward through life he goes;
Each morning sees some task begin,
    Each evening sees it close;
Something attempted, something done,
    Has earned a night's repose.

Thanks, thanks to thee, my worthy friend,
    For the lesson thou hast taught!
Thus at the flaming forge of life
    Our fortunes must be wrought;
Thus on its sounding anvil shaped
    Each burning deed and thought!

Henry Wadsworth Longfellow

Mr Skillicorn dances

Mr Skillicorn dances,
Mr Skillicorn dances,
He does it very well,
All by himself –
and when he falls,
– so slow –
he floats to the boards
on a wave of applause.

Mr Skillicorn
Falls to the floor,
'Give us some more!'
'Dance like before
you fell.'
 'Encore!'
(You can't deny he's falling well –
tonight. Yes, – this was worth waiting for.)

We laugh,
but it's not funny at all.
Not any more.

Every time he hits the stage
we all of us cackle like hell,
but it wasn't funny when
the fat comedian fell.

We laugh for him.
He falls for us.
He strips
our tears
of laughter,
We've been
falling for
years, and
– after –,
Here comes another time,
Taking its chance,
'Dance fool, dance fool,
Dance, dance, dance –'

Where's the rapport
we had before?
Mr Skillicorn you're
no longer fun.
(Outside the trains have ceased to run.)
We're willing to go home
if only you'd admit you're done.
You're old, but the moon outside is still young,
the night is still young.

Mr Skillicorn dances.

William Bealby-Wright

The Human Fly from Bendigo

My favourite uncle, Tim McFife,
Was very keen on circus life.
He had an act which stole the show –
'The Human Fly from Bendigo'.

Each night, he showed his expertise
And balanced on the high trapeze
Then, spreading both his silver wings,
He fluttered round the Roman rings.

As spotlights blazed on Uncle Tim,
A thousand eyes were fixed on him,
A phantom flying to and fro –
'The Human Fly from Bendigo'.

And so he stunned them every night,
Dressed up in foil and party lights,
Suspended by a handy wire
To keep him flying ever higher.

One dreadful night, the wire went slack
And Uncle landed on his back
But, ever faithful to his pride,
He kicked his legs, buzzed once, then died.

Doug McLeod

Bzzz . . . and the hero

Sir Basil Blazy, so I hear,
Was very handy with a spear,
He'd stop an enemy's advance
By merely flourishing a lance
And with a cannon or a gun,
He'd simply wipe out everyone!
Sir Basil Blazy, when at home,
Was fond of honey in the comb;
But if he even *heard* a bee
Buzz near him, he would rise and flee.
He'd rush upstairs, get into bed
And put a pillow on his head
Until the bee had gone away;
And then he'd come downstairs and say:
'I thought a rest would do me good,'
And go on calmly with his food.
But, knowing this, it seems to me
Sir Basil daren't face a bee,
And if he fears a thing so small
He's not a hero, after all!

Elizabeth Fleming

Why we must be heroes

'Got no guts! that's their trouble,
Do you know, when I was their age,
I'd killed twenty men stone dead.
Got no respect! that's their trouble,
Do you know, when I was their age,
You could be shot for not saluting the King's
    picture.
Got no loyalty! that's their trouble,
Always questioning our morals and ethics,
That's the trouble today,
Young people don't want to die for their country.'

C. Livesey

After Blenheim

It was a summer evening,
    Old Kaspar's work was done,
And he before his cottage door
    Was sitting in the sun;
And by him sported on the green
His little grandchild Wilhelmine.

She saw her brother Peterkin
    Roll something large and round
Which he beside the rivulet
    In playing there had found;
He came to ask what he had found
That was so large and smooth and round.

Old Kaspar took it from the boy
   Who stood expectant by;
And then the old man shook his head,
   And with a natural sigh
''Tis some poor fellow's skull,' said he,
'Who fell in the great victory.'

'I find them in the garden,
   For there's many here about;
And often when I go to plough
   The ploughshare turns them out.
For many thousand men,' said he,
'Were slain in that great victory.

'Now tell us what 'twas all about,'
   Young Peterkin he cries;
And little Wilhelmine looks up
   With wonder-waiting eyes;
'Now tell us all about the war,
And what they fought each other for.'

'It was the English,' Kaspar cried,
   'Who put the French to rout;
But what they fought each other for
   I could not well make out.
But everybody said,' quoth he,
'That 'twas a famous victory.

'My father lived at Blenheim then,
   Yon little stream hard by;
They burnt his dwelling to the ground,
   And he was forced to fly:
So with his wife and child he fled,
Nor had he where to rest his head.

'With fire and sword the country round
   Was wasted far and wide,
And many a childing mother then
   And new-born baby died:
But things like that, you know, must be
At every famous victory.

'They say it was a shocking sight
   After the field was won;
For many thousand bodies here
   Lay rotting in the sun:
But things like that, you know, must be
After a famous victory.

'Great praise the Duke of Marlbro' won
   And our good Prince Eugene';
'Why, 'twas a very wicked thing!'
   Said little Wilhelmine;
'Nay . . . nay . . . my little girl,' quoth he,
'It was a famous victory.

'And everybody praised the Duke
    Who this great fight did win.'
'But what good came of it at last?'
    Quoth little Peterkin –
'Why, that I cannot tell,' said he,
'But 'twas a famous victory.'

Robert Southey

The send–off

Down the close, darkening lanes they sang their
    way
To the siding–shed,
And lined the train with faces grimly gay.

Their breasts were stuck all white with wreath and
    spray
As men's are, dead.

Dull porters watched them, and a casual tramp
Stood staring hard,
Sorry to miss them from the upland camp.
Then, unmoved, signals nodded, and a lamp
Winked to the guard.

So secretly, like wrongs hushed–up, they went.
They were not ours:
We never heard to which front these were sent.

Nor there if they yet mock what women meant
Who gave them flowers.

Shall they return to beatings of great bells
In wild train-loads?
A few, a few, too few for drums and yells,
May creep back, silent, to still village wells
Up half-known roads.

Wilfred Owen

Armistice Day

'Stranger –
Quiet amid the tumult?
Know you not the victory won?
Hear you not the loud rejoicing?'

'Friend, I was there.'

'But the pain, the tribulation
All are gone; rejoice, rejoice!
Join the gladness of a nation,
Raise your voice!'

'But, friend, I was there.
I can hear a sweeter hymning
Through the clamour of the crowd.
And there are those whose nearest, dearest
Won but a shroud.

Not for them the shout of glory;
Nor for them the music's blare.
Thus in silence I remember –
I who was there.'

Graeme Iley

The British Grenadiers

Some talk of Alexander, and some of Hercules,
Of Conon and Lysander, and some Miltiades;
But of all the world's brave heroes, there's none that
    can compare,
With a tow, row, row, row, row, to the British
    Grenadiers.
      Chorus: But of all the world's brave heroes, etc.

None of those ancient heroes e'er saw a cannon ball,
Or knew the force of powder to slay their foes
    withal;
But our brave boys do know it, and banish all
    their fears,
With a tow, row, row, row, row, the British
    Grenadiers.
      Chorus: But our brave boys, etc.

When e'er we are commanded to storm the
    palisades,
Our leaders march with fusees and we with hand
    grenades;
We throw them from the glacis about our enemies'
    ears,
With a tow, row, row, row, row, the British
    Grenadiers.
    Chorus: We throw them, etc.

The God of War was pleased and great Bellona
    smiles,
To see these noble heroes of our British Isles;
And all the Gods celestial, descending from their
    spheres,
Beheld with admiration the British Grenadiers.
    Chorus: And all the Gods celestial, etc.

Then let us crown a bumper, and drink a health to
    those
Who carry caps and pouches, that wear the looped
    clothes;
May they and their commanders live happy all their
    years,
With a tow, row, row, row, row, the British
    Grenadiers.
    Chorus: May they and their commanders, etc.

Anon.

Said the General

Said the General of the Army,
'I think that war is barmy.'
So he threw away his gun;
Now he's having much more fun.

Spike Milligan

Colonel Fazackerley

Colonel Fazackerley Butterworth-Toast
Bought an old castle complete with a ghost,
But someone or other forgot to declare
To Colonel Fazack that the spectre was there.

On the very first evening, while waiting to dine,
The Colonel was taking a fine sherry wine,
When the ghost, with a furious flash and a flare,
Shot out of the chimney and shivered, 'Beware!'

Colonel Fazackerley put down his glass
And said, 'My dear fellow, that's really first class!
I just can't conceive how you do it at all.
I imagine you're going to a Fancy Dress Ball?'

At this, the dread ghost gave a withering cry.
Said the Colonel (his monocle firm in his eye),
'Now just how you do it I wish I could think.
Do sit down and tell me, and please have a drink.'

The ghost in his phosphorous cloak gave a roar
And floated about between ceiling and floor.
He walked through a wall and returned through a
        pane
And backed up the chimney and came down again.

Said the Colonel, 'With laughter I'm feeling quite
        weak!'
(As trickles of merriment ran down his cheek).
'My house-warming party I hope you won't spurn.
You *must* say you'll come and you'll give us a turn!'

At this, the poor spectre – quite out of his wits –
Proceeded to shake himself almost to bits.
He rattled his chains and he clattered his bones
And he filled the whole castle with mumbles and
        moans.

But Colonel Fazackerley, just as before,
Was simply delighted and called out, 'Encore!'
At which the ghost vanished, his efforts in vain,
And never was seen at the castle again.

'Oh dear, what a pity!' said Colonel Fazack.
'I don't know his name, so I can't call him back.'
And then with a smile that was hard to define,
Colonel Fazackerley went in to dine.

Charles Causley

Lucy Gray

Oft I had heard of Lucy Gray:
And when I crossed the wild,
I chanced to see at break of day
The solitary child.

No mate, no comrade Lucy knew;
She dwelt on a wide moor,
The sweetest thing that ever grew
Beside a human door!

You yet may spy the fawn at play,
The hare upon the green,
But the sweet face of Lucy Gray
Will never more be seen.

'To-night will be a stormy night –
You to the town must go;
And take a lantern, Child, to light
Your mother through the snow.'

'That, Father! will I gladly do:
'Tis scarcely afternoon –
The minster–clock has just struck two,
And yonder is the moon!'

At this the father raised his hook,
And snapped a faggot-band;
He plied his work; – and Lucy took
The lantern in her hand.

The storm came on before its time:
She wandered up and down;
And many a hill did Lucy climb:
But never reached the town.

The wretched parents all that night
Went shouting far and wide;
But there was neither sound nor sight
To serve them for a guide.

They wept – and, turning homeward, cried
'In heaven we all shall meet!'
–When in the snow the mother spied
The print of Lucy's feet.

Then downwards from the steep hill's edge
They tracked the footmarks small;
And through the broken hawthorn hedge,
And by the long stone-wall:

And then an open field they crossed,
The marks were still the same;
They tracked them on, nor ever lost;
And to the bridge they came:

They followed from the snowy bank
Those footmarks, one by one.
Into the middle of the plank;
And further there were none!

– Yet some maintain that to this day
She is a living child;
That you may see sweet Lucy Gray
Upon the lonesome wild.

O'er rough and smooth she trips along,
And never looks behind;
And sings a solitary song
That whistles in the wind.

William Wordsworth

Adventures of Isabel

Isabel met an enormous bear,
Isabel, Isabel didn't care;
The bear was hungry, the bear was ravenous,
The bear's big mouth was cruel and cavernous.
The bear said, Isabel, glad to meet you,
How do, Isabel, now I'll eat you!
Isabel, Isabel, didn't worry,
Isabel didn't scream or scurry.
She washed her hands and she straightened her hair
    up,
Then Isabel quietly ate the bear up.

Once in a night as black as pitch
Isabel met a wicked old witch.
The witch's face was cross and wrinkled,
The witch's gums with teeth were sprinkled.
Ho ho, Isabel! the old witch crowed,
I'll turn you into an ugly toad!
Isabel, Isabel, didn't worry,
Isabel didn't scream or scurry,
She showed no rage and she showed no rancour,
But she turned the witch into milk and drank her.

Isabel met a hideous giant,
Isabel continued self-reliant.
The giant was hairy, the giant was horrid,
He had one eye in the middle of his forehead.
Good morning, Isabel, the giant said,
I'll grind your bones to make my bread.
Isabel, Isabel, didn't worry,
Isabel didn't scream or scurry.
She nibbled the zwieback that she always fed off,
And when it was gone, she cut the giant's head off.

Isabel met a troublesome doctor,
He punched and he poked till he really shocked her.
The doctor's talk was of coughs and chills
And the doctor's satchel bulged with pills.
The doctor said unto Isabel,
Swallow this it will make you well.
Isabel, Isabel, didn't worry,
Isabel didn't scream or scurry.
She took those pills from the pill concocter,
And Isabel calmly cured the doctor.

Ogden Nash

from 'The Women of Mumbles Head'

Up at a lighthouse window two women beheld the
   storm,
And saw in the boiling breakers a figure – a fighting
   form,
It might be the grey-haired father – then the women
   held their breath,
It might be a fair-haired brother, who was having a
   round with death;
It might be a lover, a husband, whose kisses were on
   the lips
Of the women whose love is the life of men going
   down to the sea in ships;
They had seen the launch of the lifeboat, they had
   heard the worst, and more;
Then, kissing each other, these women went down
   from the lighthouse, straight to shore.

There by the rocks on the breakers these sisters,
    hand in hand,
Beheld once more that desperate man who
    struggled to reach the land.
'Twas only aid he wanted to help him across the
    wave,
But what are a couple of women with only a man to
    save?
What are a couple of women? Well, more than three
    craven men
Who stood by the shore with chattering teeth,
    refusing to stir – and then
Off went the women's shawls, sir; in a second
    they're torn and rent,
And knotting them into a rope of love, straight into
    the sea they went!

'Come back,' cried the lighthouse-keeper, 'for
    God's sake, girls, come back!'
As they caught the waves on their foreheads,
    resisting the fierce attack.
'Come back!' moaned the grey-haired mother, as
    she stood by the angry sea,
'If the waves take you, my darlings, there's nobody
    left to me.'

'Come back!' said the three strong soldiers, who still
    stood faint and pale,
'You will drown if you face the breakers! you will
    fall if you brave the gale!'
'Come back!' said the girls, 'we will not! go tell it to
    all the town,
We'll lose our lives, God willing, before that man
    shall drown!

Give one more knot to the shawls, Bess! give one
    strong clutch of your hand!
Just follow me, brave, to the shingle, and we'll
    bring him safe to land!
Wait for the next wave, darling, only a minute
    more,
And I'll have him safe in my arms, dear, and we'll
    drag him safe to shore.'
Up their arms in the water, fighting it breast to
    breast,
They caught and saved a brother alive! God bless us,
    you know the rest.
Well, many a heart beat stronger, and many a tear
    was shed,
And many a glass was toss'd right off to 'The
    Women of Mumbles Head!'

Clement Scott

George and the dragonfly

Georgie Jennings was spit almighty.
When the golly was good
he could down a dragonfly at 30 feet
and drown a 100 midges with the fallout.
At the drop of a cap
he would outspit lads
years older and twice his size.
Freckled and rather frail
he assumed the quiet dignity
beloved of schoolboy heroes.

But though a legend in his own playtime
Georgie Jennings failed miserably in the classroom
    and left school at 15 to work for his father.
And talents such as spitting
are considered unbefitting
for upandcoming porkbutchers.

I haven't seen him since,
but like to imagine some summer soirée
when, after a day moistening mince,
George and his wife entertain tanned friends.
And after dinner, sherrytongued talk
drifts back to schooldays
The faces halfrecalled, the adventures
overexaggerated. And the next thing
that shy sharpshooter of days gone by
    is led, vainly protesting, on to the lawn
where, in the hush of a golden august evening
a reputation, 20 years tall, is put to the test.
So he takes extra care as yesterheroes must,
fires, and a dragonfly, encapsulated, bites the dust.
Then amidst bravos and tinkled applause,
blushing, Georgie leads them back indoors.

Roger McGough

Saint George and the Dragon

Saint George he slew the dragon,
    But he didn't shout hurray.
He dumped it in the wagon
    Just to clear the mess away.

But the wagoner he sold it
    To a showman at the fair
And when Saint George was told it,
    He was almost in despair.

For the people crowded round it
    To admire its teeth and claws,
But Saint George he was an Englishman
    And did not like applause.

'The creechah weighed a ton at most,'
    He muttered through his vizahd,
'I do not feel inclined to boast
    About that puny lizahd.'

Alfred Noyes

The Lambton Worm
(A North Country folk tale)

One Sunday mornin' Lambton went
A-fishin' in the Wear;
An' catched a fish upon his hook
He thought looked varry queer.
But what'n kind of fish it was
Young Lambton couldn't tell
He wasn't fashed to carry it hame,
So he hoyed ot in a well.

    Whisht, lads, haad yor gobs,
    I'll tell ye all an awful story
    Whisht, lads, haad yor gobs,
    I'll tell ye 'bout the worm.

Now Lambton felt inclined to go
An' fight in foreign wars.
He joined a troop of knights that cared
For neither wounds nor scars.
An' off he went to Palestine
Where queer things him befell,
An' varry soon forgot about
The queer worm in the well.

But the worm got fat, an' growed, an' growed,
An' growed an awful size,
With great big teeth, a great big gob,
An' great big goggly eyes.
An' when at night he crawled about
To pick up bits of news,
If he felt thirsty on the road
He'd milk a dozen coos.

This fearful worm would often feed
On calves an' lambs an' sheep,
An' swallow little bairns alive
When they lay down to sleep.
An' when he'd eaten all he could
An' he had had his fill,
He crawled away and lapped his tail
Ten times round Penshaw Hill.

The news of this most awful worm
An' his queer gannins on
Soon crossed the seas, got to the ears
Of brave and bold Sir John.
So home he came an' catched the beast
An' cut him in two halves,
And that soon stopped his eatin' bairns
An' sheep, an' lambs, an' calves.

So now ye know how all the folks
On both sides of the Wear
Lost lots of sheep an' lots of sleep
An' lived in mortal fear.
So let's have one to brave Sir John
Who kept the bairns from harm,
Saved coos an' calves by makin' halves
Of the famous Lambton Worm.

Now, lads, I'll haad me gob,
That's all I know about the story
Of Sir John's clever job
With the awful Lambton Worm.

Anon.

It couldn't be done

Somebody said that it couldn't be done,
But he, with a grin, replied
He'd never be one to say it couldn't be done –
Leastways, not till he'd tried.
So he buckled right in, with a trace of a grin,
By golly, he went right to it.
He tackled The Thing That Couldn't Be Done!
And he couldn't do it.

Anon.

Harold's leap

Harold, are you asleep?
Harold, I remember your leap;
It may have killed you
But it was a brave thing to do.
Two promontories ran high into the sky;
He leapt from one rock to the other
And fell to the sea's smother.
Harold was always afraid to climb high,
But something urged him on;
He felt he should try.
I would not say that he was wrong,
Although he succeeded in doing nothing but die.
Would you?
Ever after, that steep
Place was called Harold's Leap.
It was a brave thing to do.

Stevie Smith

The tunnel

This is the way that I have to go
I've left all my friends behind
Back there, where a faint light glimmers
Round the long tunnel's bend.

I can't see a roof up above me,
I can't find either wall,
My shoes slip on the slimy boulders -
How far is it down, if I fall?

Beneath me the same stream is flowing
That laughed in the fields back there –
Here, it is black, like the leeches and weeds,
And the bats flitting through the dank air.

It's just the same if I shut my eyes;
My companions, all around,
Are trickles, drips, sploshes, sudden plops.
Then a strange, sucking sound.

One shoe's full of the cold dark water,
My hands slither over the stones.
My throat's gone dry, my heart pound-pounds,
but I can only go on—

Till I can see them, they can see me
and again they start to shout,
The rats bite, watch out for the rats
But now I am almost out.

Dizzy, happy, I blink at the light.
The sun's still shining, the birds still sing,
Someone is patting me on the back –
Now I am one of the gang.

Brian Lee

My parents kept me from children who who were rough

My parents kept me from children who were rough
And who threw words like stones and who wore
   torn clothes.
Their thighs showed through rags. They ran in the
   street
And climbed cliffs and stripped by the country
   streams.
I feared more than tigers their muscles like iron
And their jerking hands and their knees tight on my
   arms.
I feared the salt coarse pointing of those boys
Who copied my lisp behind me on the road.

They were lithe, they sprang out behind hedges
Like dogs to bark at our world. They threw mud
And I looked another way, pretending to smile.
I longed to forgive them, yet they never smiled.

Stephen Spender

To show it so

what a burnin inna man flesh
wid a whorlin an a turnin giddy in de head
when de snap whey ring out crack as dough of bone
at de flight of whip as lash slash flesh;
an de sun did startle harsh an red
when sting dat sing did bring
man an man whey straight inna grace an toil
to crash in a twis like a shadow fallin sudden doun
   so.

O dat it shud be so kanstant!
why mus de stings everlastin stay be so?

to know dat hurt . . . to know it
to know dat hurt an to show it.

got to hold it doun dey, dough yu feeling got to
    show,
O ye sons an dautas of affliction, O ye warriyahs be,
till yu site de rite time for de go to make a show
an deliver yu blow so fierce to pierce de wicked O;
for it shall come to pass dat swords an spears shall
    cross.
de wicked, even they dat do evil unto you,
shall feel de wrath of man an man an they shall not
    be.
soh hold it doun dey; mek it ripe fe de time dat is
    rite.

Linton Kwesi Johnson

I've got an apple ready

My hair's tightly plaited;
I've a bright blue bow;
I don't want my breakfast,
And now I must go.

My satchel's on my shoulder;
Nothing's out of place;
And I've got an apple ready,
Just in case.

So it's 'Goodbye, Mother!'
And off down the street!
Briskly at first
On pit–a–pat feet,

But slow and more slow
As I reach the tarred
Trackway that runs
By Hodson's Yard;

For it's there sometimes
Bill Craddock waits for me
To snatch off my beret
And throw it in a tree.

Bill Craddock is leaning
On Hodson's rails;
Bill with thin hands
And dirty nails;

Bill with a front tooth
Broken and bad;
His dark eyes cruel,
And somewhat sad.

Often there are workmen,
And then he doesn't dare;
But this morning I feel
He'll be there.

At the corner he will pounce . . .
But quickly I'll say
'Hallo, Bill, have an apple!' –
In an ordinary way.

I'll push it in his hand
And walk right on;
And when I'm round the corner
I'll run.

John Walsh

Coming home

It's not really scary
when you come in the house
and nobody's there

　　　it's just

that the chairs seem to
stare
and the room looks so big and
the deep sounds of quiet
make a buzz in your ears

　　　and

Mum'll be back soon
it's really all right
the teapot's all ready,
I'm not at all frightened
I'll switch on the TV
but not for a minute

I'll just sit here
I don't want to move from the chair
and it's not really scary
I'm not at all frightened
and only a *Baby* would start to believe
that something invisible's
sitting behind

I'll look in a minute
Yes, that's what I'll do
in a minute I'll look

I'll just sit here
and soon I'll switch on
the TV
in a minute or two
it's only a box – after all
just a box and I know that
it can't really whisper
those horrible things
when it isn't switched on

     cos

I'm old enough now
Yes, I'm old enough now and
I don't really mind
No, I don't really mind
cos

  it's only till Six

Mick Gowar

The King of the Crocodiles

'Now, woman, why without your veil?
And wherefore do you look so pale?
And, woman, why do you groan so sadly,
And wherefore beat your bosom madly?'

'Oh, I have lost my darling child,
And that's the loss that makes me wild;
He stoop'd by the river down to drink,
And there was a Crocodile by the brink.

He did not venture in to swim,
He only stoop'd to drink at the brim;
But under the reeds the Crocodile lay,
And struck with his tail and swept him away.

Now take me in your boat, I pray,
For down the river lies my way,
And me to the Reed Island bring,
For I will go to the Crocodile King.

And to the King I will complain
How my poor child was wickedly slain;
The King of Crocodiles he is good,
And I shall have the murderer's blood.'

The man replied, 'No, woman, no;
To the Island of Reeds I will not go;
I would not for any worldly thing
See the face of the Crocodile King.'

'Then lend me now your little boat,
And I will down the river float,
I tell thee that no worldly thing
Shall keep me from the Crocodile King.'

The woman she leapt into the boat,
And down the river alone did she float,
And fast with the stream the boat proceeds,
And now she is come to the Island of Reeds.

The King of the Crocodiles there was seen;
He sat upon the eggs of the Queen,
And all around, a numerous rout,
The young Prince Crocodiles crawl'd about.

She fell upon her bended knee,
And said, 'O King, have pity on me,
For I have lost my darling child,
And that's the loss that makes me wild.

A crocodile ate him for his food:
Now let me have the murderer's blood;
Let me have vengeance for my boy,
The only thing that can give me joy.

I know that you, sire, never do wrong,
You have no tail so stiff and strong,
You have no tail to strike and slay,
But you have ears to hear what I say.'

'You have done well,' the king replies,
And fix'd on her his little eyes;
'Good woman, yes, you have done right;
But you have not described me quite.

I have no tail to strike and slay,
And I have ears to hear what you say;
I have teeth, moreover, as you may see,
And I will make a meal of thee.'

'A meal of me!' the woman cried,
Taking wit in her anger, and courage beside;
She took him his forelegs and hind between
And trundled him off the eggs of the Queen.

Two Crocodile Princes, as they played on the sand,
She caught, and grasping them one in each hand,
Thrust the head of one into the throat of the other,
And made each Prince Crocodile choke his brother.

And when she had trussed three couple this way,
She carried them off and hastened away,
And plying her oars with might and main,
Crossed the river and got to the shore again.

When the Crocodile Queen came home, she found
That her eggs were broken and scattered around,
And that six young princes, darlings all,
Were missing; for none of them answered her call.

Then many a not very pleasant thing
Passed between her and the Crocodile King;
'Is this your care of the nest?' cried she;
'It comes of your gadding abroad,' said he.

The Queen had the better in this dispute,
And the Crocodile King found it best to be mute;
While a terrible peal in his ears she rung,
For the Queen had a tail as well as a tongue.

The woman, meantime, was very well pleased,
She had saved her life, and her heart was eased;
The justice she asked in vain for her son,
She had taken herself, and six for one.

'Mash–Allah!' her neighbours exclaimed in delight,
She gave them a funeral supper that night,
Where they all agreed that revenge was sweet,
And young Prince Crocodiles delicate meat.

Robert Southey

Taught me purple

My mother taught me purple
    Although she never wore it.
Wash–grey was her circle,
    The tenement her orbit.

My mother taught me golden
    And held me up to see it,
Above the broken molding,
    Beyond the filthy street.

My mother reached for beauty
    And for its lack she died,
Who knew so much of duty
    She could not teach me pride.

Evelyn Tooley Hunt

Capstan bars

'We were much relieved, when dawn broke, to see
our boat beating home on the offing. As there had
been no news of her all night some of us had feared
that she might have been overwhelmed. There was
still a very heavy surf and I judged it necessary to
engage extra helpers. Most of the women launchers
had been up all night and looked tired, and it was
essential to get the boat out of the surf as quick as
possible.'

— Honorary Secretary's Report

Come ladies, man the capstan bars,
Capstan bars, the capstan bars,
Come ladies, man the capstan bars
And warp your husbands in.

Most of you women 'ave spent the night,
Terrible night, oh a dirty night,
Watching an' waitin' for mornin' light,
To know will ever they come.

Screechin' voice of the south–east gale,
South–east gale, a proper gale,
Scream an' roar wi' answerin' wail
An' they in the tumblin' foam.

Crash an' send the salt sea waves,
Salt sea waves, great green back waves,
Breakers ravin' for seamen's graves,
Murmurin' Davy Jones.

Hours of darkness creepin' by,
Slowly creepin', creepin' by,
Flush o' dawn in the weather sky,
An' then the watch is done.

So merrily heave, the capstan bars,
The capstan bars, the capstan bars,
Ho merrily heave the capstan bars
An' welcome life–boat home.

Captain Q. Craufurd, R.N.,ret.

Living among the toilers

I live among workers
Where life ebbs in shadows
And see waning petals
In the depths of children's eyes.

I share the conveyor belt –
And feel the iron wheel
Ride my bones,
Crushing.

I hear the cry
Of the cheated
And add my fist,
Accusing.

My vision clear,
I sing
Of a chromed tomorrow
Held in my calloused palm.

Henri Percikow

A poem of John Fontaine

I try to get the workers to strike
My name is John Fontaine,
I climbed right up to the top
Of my big 100-foot-high crane.

Look at all those people
Standing on the ground,
I'm so high up in my cock-pit
I cannot hear a sound.

I'm up here in my crane,
My hungry belly is like a bump,
But I'm up here fellow unionists
To go against the lump.

Chris Looker (11)

In the mine

Down in the mine
It's a dirty old place
Where miners work
To earn their place.

Down at seven
Out at four,
At fifty-five
They can work no more.

Bones are broke
The body is crushed
Then they are left
Like godridden dust.

'Get on, get on,'
Are the foreman's words,
'More coal, more money,'
It's the motto he's learned.

Then 'NO' say the miners
Up in revolt,
Stand as one
And together we'll vote.

Fight for more money,
Fight for their rights,
'We're only human beings,
We deserve better rights.'

Michael Rose (14)

The dying gladiator

I see before me the gladiator lie:
　He leans upon his hand – his manly brow
　Consents to death, but conquers agony,
　And his drooped head sinks gradually low —
　And through his side the last drops, ebbing slow
　From the red gash, fall heavy, one by one,
　Like the first of a thunder-shower; and now
　The arena swims around him – he is gone,
Ere ceased the inhuman shout which hailed the
　wretch who won.

He heard it, but he heeded not – his eyes
　Were with his heart and that was far away;
　He recked not of the life he lost nor prize,
　But where his rude hut by the Danube lay,
　There were his young barbarians all at play,
　There was their Dacian mother – he, their sire,
　Butchered to make a Roman holiday —
　All this rushed with his blood – Shall he expire
And unavenged? – Arise! ye Goths, and glut your
　ire!

Lord Byron

The ballad of Billy Rose

Outside Bristol Rovers Football Ground –
The date has gone from me, but not the day,
Nor how the dissenting flags in stiff array
Struck bravely out against the grey sky's round –

Near the Car Park then, past Austin and Ford,
Lagonda, Bentley, and a colourful patch
Of contrary coaches come in for the match,
Was where I walked, having travelled the road

From Fishponds to watch Portsmouth in the Cup.
The Third Round, I believe. And I was filled
With the old excitement which had thrilled
Me so completely when, while growing up,

I went on Saturdays to match or fight.
Not only me; for thousands of us there
Strode forward eagerly, each man aware
Of vigorous memory, anticipating delight.

We all marched forward, all, except one man.
I saw him because he was paradoxically still,
A stone against the flood, face upright against us all,
Head bare, hoarse voice aloft. Blind as a stone.

I knew him at once despite his pathetic clothes;
Something in his stance, or his sturdy frame
Perhaps. I could even remember his name
Before I saw it on the blind-man's tray. Billy Rose.

And twenty forgetful years fell away at the sight.
Bare-kneed, dismayed, memory fled to the hub
Of Saturday violence, with friends to the Labour
   Club
Watching the boxing on a sawdust summer night.

The boy's enclosure close to the shabby ring
Was where we stood, clenched in a resin world,
Spoke in cool voices, lounged, were artificially
   bored
During minor bouts. We paid threepence to go in.

Billy Rose fought there. He was top of the bill,
So brisk a fighter, so gallant, so precise!
Trim as a tree he stood for the ceremonies,
Then turned to meet George Moran of Triphil.

He had no chance. Courage was not enough,
Nor tight defence. Donald Davies was sick –
We threatened his cowardice with an embarrassed
   kick.
Ripped across both eyes was Rose, but we were
   tough

And clapped him as they wrapped his blindness up
In busy towels, applauding the wave
He gave the executioner, cheered the brave
Blind man as he cleared with a jaunty hop

The top rope. I had forgotten the day
As if it were dead for ever, yet now I saw
The flowers of punched blood on the ring floor
As bright as his name. I do not know

How long I stood with ghosts of the wild fists
And cries of shaken boys long dead around me,
For stuck to act at last, in terror and pity
I threw some frantic money, three treacherous
    pence

(I cry at the memory) into his tray, and ran,
Entering the waves of the stadium like a drowning
    man.
Poor Billy Rose. God, he could fight
Before my three sharp coins knocked out his sight.

Leslie Norris

On his blindness

When I consider how my light is spent
Ere half my days in this dark world and wide,
And that one talent which is death to hide,
Lodged with me useless, though my soul more bent
To serve there with my Maker, and present
My true account, lest he, returning, chide;
'Doth God exact day-labour, light denied?'
I fondly ask: but Patience, to prevent
That murmur, soon replies, 'God doth not need
Either man's work, or his own gifts; who best
Bear his mild yoke, they serve him best; his state
Is kingly: thousands at his bidding speed,
And post o'er land and ocean without rest;
They also serve who only stand and wait.'

John Milton

Billy Medals

Do you know Billy Medals
That warrior bold,
His stars made of silver,
His circles of gold?
O there don't seem a battle
Of land, sea or air
For fifty years past
But old Bill wasn't there.

He stands on the corner
As straight as a gun,
And his circles and stars
Catch the rays of the sun.
His stars and his circles
All glitter and gleam,
And just like the rainbow
His ribbons they beam.

You must know Billy Medals
With his chestful of gongs,
He knows all the war-stories
And all the war-songs.
His jacket is ragged
His trousers are green,
And no one stands straighter
For 'God Save the Queen'.

Around his torn topper
Are badges in scores
Of goodness knows how many
Different corps.
But in war Billy Medals
Has never known harm
For he's never been farther
Than Fiveacre Farm.

When lads from the village
Dodged shrapnel and shell,
Billy Medals was cleaning out
Wishworthy Well.
When in deserts they sweated,
In oceans they froze,
Billy Medals was scaring
The rooks and the crows.

Did you see the brave soldier
New-home from the war
Give Billy the star
That once proudly he bore?
Billy Medals he cackled
And capered with glee
And the village-boys laughed,
But the soldier not he.

Charles Causley

Faithless Nelly Gray

Ben Battle was a soldier bold,
    And used to war's alarms:
But a cannon-ball took off his legs,
    So he laid down his arms!

Now as they bore him off the field,
    Said he, 'Let others shoot,
For here I leave my second leg,
    And the Forty-second Foot!'

Now Ben he loved a pretty maid,
    Her name was Nelly Gray;
So he went to pay her his devours
    When he'd devoured his pay!

But when he called on Nelly Gray,
    She made him quite a scoff;
And when she saw his wooden legs,
    Began to take them off!

Said she, 'I loved a soldier once,
    For he was blithe and brave;
But I will never love a man
    With both legs in the grave!

Before you had those timber toes,
    Your love I did allow,
But then, you know, you stand upon
    Another footing now!'

'O Nelly Gray! O Nelly Gray!
    For all your jeering speeches,
At duty's call I left my legs
    In Badajos's *breeches*!'

'Why, then,' said she, 'you've lost the feet
    Of legs in war's alarms,
And now you cannot wear your shoes
    Upon your feats of arms!'

'O, false and fickle Nelly Gray;
    I know why you refuse: –
Though I've no feet – some other man
    Is standing in my shoes!

I wish I ne'er had seen your face;
    But, now, a long farewell!
For you will be my death; – alas!
    You will not be my *Nell*!'

So round his melancholy neck
    A rope he did entwine,
And for his second time in life,
    Enlisted in the Line!

One end he tied around a beam,
    And then removed his pegs,
And, as his legs were off, – of course,
    He soon was off his legs!

And there he hung till he was dead
    As any nail in town, –
For though distress had cut him up,
    It could not cut him down!

Thomas Hood

I know a man who's got a pebble

I know a man who's got a pebble.
He found it and he sucked it
during the war
He found it and he sucked it
when they ran out of water
He found it and he sucked it
when they were dying for a drink.
and he sucked it and he sucked it
for days and days and days.

I know a man who's got a pebble
and he keeps it in his drawer

It's small and brown – nothing much to look at
but I think of the things he thinks
when he sees it:
how he found it
how he sucked it
how he nearly died for water to drink.

A small brown pebble
tucked under his tongue
and he keeps it in his drawer
to look at now and then.

Michael Rosen

With the life-boat crew

A shrieking sky and a wind-torn sea –
   Steadily lads!
And sheltered under the Life-boat's lee –
   Steadily lads!
Storm-marked faces and shaggy hair,
   Jackets of rusty blue,
Men who will do and will not despair –
   Men of the Life-boat crew.

The flash of a flare; the rocket's flight –
    Steadily lads!
A cry of distress across the night –
    Steadily lads!
Over the sands with rush and shout,
    Facing the biting spray;
Hurrah! she's afloat and out-and-out,
    Staunchly my men give way.

Tottering spars and splintering deck –
    Steadily lads!
A mad sea covered with floating wreck –
    Steadily lads!
Fighting with death up under her lee –
    'Ready there in the bow,
Cast as she lifts to the next long sea –
    Cast! Ah, we have her now!'

Jump my lads while your vessel holds –
    Steadily lads!
Into the boat ere the next sea folds –
    Steadily lads!
Have we you all? Watch the spar!
    Quick! out the grapnel clear.
We sweep ashore, there's a grinding jar;
    Hark to our messmates cheer.

Up with the boat on her wheels again –
    Steadily lads!
Back to our watch of the darkened main –
    Steadily lads!
Ever ready to dare and to do,
    Sons of the Vikings we!
We are the men of the Life-boat crew,
    The children of the sea!

W. Watt

The ship

There was no song nor shout of joy
    Nor beam of moon or sun,
When she came back from the voyage
    Long ago begun;
But twilight on the waters
    Was quiet and grey,
And she glided steady, steady and pensive,
    Over the open bay.

Her sails were brown and ragged,
    And her crew hollow-eyed,
But their silent lips spoke content
    And their shoulders pride;
Though she had no captives on her deck,
    And in her hold
There were no heaps of corn or timber
    Or silks or gold.

J. C. Squire

Daniel

Darius the Mede was a king and a wonder.
His eye was proud, and his voice was thunder.
He kept bad lions in a monstrous den.
He fed up the lions on Christian men.
Daniel was the chief hired man of the land.
He stirred up the music in the palace band.
He whitewashed the cellar. He shovelled in the coal.
And Daniel kept a-praying: – 'Lord save my soul.'
Daniel kept a-praying: – 'Lord save my soul.'
Daniel kept a-praying: – 'Lord save my soul.'

Daniel was the butler, swagger and swell.
He ran up stairs. He answered the bell.
And *he* would let in whoever came a-calling: –
Saints so holy, scamps so appalling.
'Old man Ahab leaves his card.
Elisha and the bears are a-waiting in the yard.
Here comes Pharaoh and his snakes a-calling.
Here comes Cain and his wife a-calling.
Shadrach, Meschach and Abednego for tea.
Here comes Jonah and the whale,
And the *Sea*!
Here comes St Peter and his fishing pole.
Here comes Judas and his silver a-calling.
Here comes old Beelzebub a-calling.'
And Daniel kept a-praying: – 'Lord save my soul.'
Daniel kept a-praying: – 'Lord save my soul.'
Daniel kept a-praying: – 'Lord save my soul.'

His sweetheart and his mother were Christian and
    meek.
They washed and ironed for Darius every week.
One Thursday he met them at the door: –
Paid them as usual, but acted sore.
He said:– 'Your Daniel is a dead little pigeon.
He's a good hard worker, but he talks religion.'
And he showed them Daniel in the lion's cage.
Daniel standing quietly, the lions in a rage.
His good old mother cried: –
'Lord save him.'
And Daniel's tender sweetheart cried: –
'Lord save him.'
And she was a golden lily in the dew.
And she was as sweet as an apple on the tree.
And she was as fine as a melon in the corn-field,
Gliding and lovely as a ship on the sea,
Gliding and lovely as a ship on the sea.

And she prayed to the Lord: –
'Send Gabriel, Send Gabriel.'

King Darius said to the lions: –
'Bite Daniel, Bite Daniel.
Bite him. Bite him. Bite him!'

Thus roared the lions: –
'We want Daniel, Daniel, Daniel,
We want Daniel, Daniel, Daniel.
Grrrrrrrrrrrrrrrrrrrrrrrrrrrrrrrrrrrrrrrrrrrr
Grrrrrrrrrrrrrrrrrrrrrrrrrrrrrrrrrrrrrrrrrrrrr.

And Daniel did not frown.
Daniel did not cry.
He kept on looking at the sky.
And the Lord said to Gabriel: –
'Go chain the lions down,
Go chain the lions down.
Go chain the lions down.
Go chain the lions down.'

And Gabriel chained the lions,
And Gabriel chained the lions,
And Gabriel chained the lions,

And Daniel got out of the den,
And Daniel got out of the den,
And Daniel got out of the den.
And Darius said: – 'You're a Christian child,'
Darius said: – 'You're a Christian child,'
And gave him his job again,
And gave him his job again,
And gave him his job again.

Vachel Lindsay

Landing of the Pilgrim Fathers

The breaking waves dashed high,
    On a stern and rock-bound coast,
And the woods against a storm sky,
    Their giant branches tossed.

And the heavy night hung dark,
    The hills and waters o'er,
When a band of exiles moored their bark
    On the wild New England shore.

Not as the conqueror comes,
    They, the true-hearted came;
Not with the roll of the stirring drums,
    And the trumpet that sings of fame.

Not as the flying come,
    In silence and in fear –
They shook the depths of the desert gloom
    With their hymns of lofty cheer.

Amidst the storm they sang,
    And the stars heard, and the sea;
And the sounding aisles of the dim woods rang
    To the anthem of the free.

The ocean eagle soared
    From his nest by the white wave's foam;
And the rocking pines of the forest roared –
    This was their welcome home.

There were men with hoary hair
    Amidst that pilgrim band:
Why had they come to wither there,
    Away from their childhood's land?

There was a woman's fearless eye,
    Lit by her deep love's truth;
There was manhood's brow serenely high,
    And the fiery heart of youth.

What sought they thus afar?
    Bright jewels of the mine?
The wealth of seas, the spoils of war?
    They sought a faith's pure shrine!

Aye, call it holy ground,
    The soil where first they trod;
They have left unstained what there they found –
    Freedom to worship God.

Felicia Hemans

Gawain and the Green Knight

One New Year's Day a giant knight, dressed all in
green, arrived at the Court of King Arthur and
challenged Sir Gawain to strike him one blow and to
receive one in return. Gawain cut off the giant's
head – but the giant simply picked it up and put it
back on again. As he rode away he told Gawain that
he must meet him to fulfil the second part of their
bargain in exactly one year's time. Next New Year's

Day the two met again, and Sir Gawain stood
before the Green Knight, waiting bravely to receive
his blow.

'Be brisk, man, by your faith, and bring me to the
     point;
Deal me my destiny and do it out of hand,
For I shall stand your stroke, not starting at all
Till your axe has hit me. Here is my oath on it.'
'Have at you then!' said the other, heaving up his
     axe,
Behaving as angrily as if he were mad.
He menaced him mightily, but made no contact,
Smartly withholding his hand without hurting him.
Gawain waited unswerving, with not a wavering
     limb,
But stood still as a stone or the stump of a tree
Gripping the rocky ground with a hundred
     grappling roots.
Then again the Green Knight began to gird:
'So now you have a whole heart I must hit you.
May the high knighthood which Arthur conferred
Preserve you and save your neck, if so it avail you!'
Then said Gawain, storming with sudden rage,
'Thrash on, you thrustful fellow, you threaten too
     much.
It seems your spirit is struck with self-dread.'
'Forsooth,' the other said, 'you speak so fiercely
I will no longer lengthen matters by delaying your
     business,
               I vow.'
     He stood astride to smite,
     Lips pouting, puckered brow.
     No wonder he lacked delight
     Who expected no help now.

Up went the axe at once and hurtled down straight
At the naked neck with its knife-like edge.
Though it swung down savagely, slight was the
    wound,
A mere snick on the side, so that the skin was
    broken.
Through the fair fat to the flesh fell the blade,
And over his shoulders the shimmering blood shot
    to the ground.
When Sir Gawain saw his gore glinting on the
    snow,
He leapt feet close together a spear's length away,
Hurriedly heaved his helmet on to his head,
And shrugging his shoulders, shot his shield to the
    front,
Swung out his bright sword and said fiercely,
(For never had the knight since being nursed by his
    mother
Been so buoyantly happy, so blithe in this world)
'Cease your blows, sir, strike me no more.
I have sustained a stroke here unresistingly,

And if you offer any more I shall earnestly reply.
Resisting, rest assured, with the most rancorous
  Despite.
  The single stroke is wrought
  To which we pledged our plight
  In high King Arthur's court:
  Enough now, therefore, knight!'

Anon.

The ballad of postman William L. Moore from Baltimore

who marched on his own into the Southern States in 1963.
He protested against the persecution of the negroes.
He was shot after a week.
Three bullets struck his forehead.

SUNDAY
Sunday meant rest for William L. Moore
after a hard week's work.
He was only a postman and pretty poor,
he came from Baltimore.

MONDAY
Monday, one day in Baltimore,
he said to Mrs Moore:
I don't want to be a postman no more,
I'm going down south on a tour.
  BLACK AND WHITE, UNITE! UNITE!
  on a placard he wrote.
  White and black – hold repression back!
  And he set off on his own.

TUESDAY
Tuesday, one day on the railway train,
people asked William L. Moore
what was the sign he was carrying,
and wished him luck for his tour.
    BLACK AND WHITE, UNITE! UNITE!
    stood on his placard . . .

WEDNESDAY
Wednesday, one day in Alabama,
walking down the main street,
still a long way from Birmingham,
he'd already got aching feet.
    BLACK AND WHITE, UNITE! UNITE!

THURSDAY
Thursday, the day the sheriff stopped him,
said, 'What the hell – you're white!
What business of yours is the niggers, man?
If it's trouble you want – all right!'
    BLACK AND WHITE, UNITE! UNITE!

FRIDAY
Friday, a dog started following him,
became his only friend.
By evening stones were hitting them both,
but they went on to the end.
    BLACK AND WHITE, UNITE! UNITE!

SAT'DAY
Sat'day, that day it was terribly hot,
a white woman came up to the two,
gave him a drink and secretly whispered:
'I think the same as you.'
    BLACK AND WHITE, UNITE! UNITE!

LAST DAY

Sunday, a blue and summer's day,
he lay in the grass so green —
three red carnations blooming blood–red
on his forehead could be seen.

BLACK AND WHITE UNITE! UNITE!
Stood on his placard.
White and black – hold repression back!
And he died on his own.
And he won't be alone.

Wolf Biermann
(TRANSLATED FROM THE GERMAN BY STEVE GOOCH)

A dream of hanging

He rang me up
In a dream,
My brother did.
He had been hanged
That morning,
Innocent,
And I had slept
Through the striking
Of the clock
While it had taken place,
Eight,
Just about time enough
For it to happen.
He spoke to me
On the telephone
That afternoon
To reassure me,
My dear brother
Who had killed nobody,
And I asked him,
Long distance,
What it had felt like
To be hanged.
'Oh, don't worry, lovey,' he said,
'When your time comes.
It tickled rather.'

Patricia Beer

Lines said to have been written on the eve of his execution

Even such is Time, which takes in trust
Our youth, our joys, and all we have,
And pays us but with age and dust,
Which in the dark and silent grave,
When we have wandered all our ways,
Shuts up the story of our days:
  But from this earth, this grave, this dust,
  The Lord shall raise me up, I trust.

Walter Raleigh

A ballad of Hell

'A letter from my love today!
  Oh, unexpected, dear appeal!'
She struck a happy tear away,
  And broke the crimson seal.

The colour died from out her face,
  Her eyes like ghostly candles shone;
She cast dread looks about the place,
  Then clenched her teeth and read right on.

'I may not pass the prison door;
    Here must I rot from day to day,
Unless I wed whom I abhor,
    My cousin, Blanche of Valencay.

At midnight with my dagger keen,
    I'll take my life; it must be so.
Meet me in Hell tonight, my queen,
    For weal and woe.'

She waited, shuddering in her room,
    Till sleep had fallen on all the house.
She never flinched; she faced her doom:
    They two must sin to keep their vows.

Without a pause she bared her breast,
    And drove her dagger home and fell,
And lay like one that takes her rest,
    And died and wakened up in Hell.

The devil started at her side,
    Comely, and tall, and black as jet.
'I am young Malespina's bride;
    Has he come hither yet?'

'My poppet, welcome to your bed.'
    'Is Malespina here?'
'Not he! Tomorrow he must wed
    His cousin Blanche, my dear!'

'You lie, he died with me tonight.'
    'Not he! it was a plot . . .' 'You lie.'
'My dear, I never lie outright.'
    'We died at midnight, he and I.'

The devil went. Without a groan
    She, gathered up in one fierce prayer,
Took root in Hell's midst all alone,
    And waited for him there.

How long she stayed I cannot tell;
    But when she felt his perfidy,
She marched across the floor of Hell;
    And all the damned stood up to see.

The devil stopped her at the brink:
    She shook him off; she cried, 'Away!'
'My dear, you have gone mad, I think.'
    'I was betrayed: I will not stay.'

Across the weltering deep she ran;
    A stranger thing was never seen:
The damned stood silent to a man;
    They saw the great gulf set between.

To her it seemed a meadow fair;
    And flowers sprang up about her feet.
She entered heaven; she climbed the stair
    And knelt down at the mercy-seat.

Seraphs and saints with one great voice
    Welcomed that soul that knew not fear.
Amazed to find it could rejoice,
    Hell raised a hoarse, half-human cheer.

John Davidson

The dog

The dog was there, outside her door,
   She gave it food and drink,
She gave it shelter from the cold:
   It was the night young Molly robbed
An old fool of his gold.

'Molly,' I said, 'you'll go to hell —'
   And yet I half believed
That ugly, famished, tottering cur
   Would bark outside the gates of Heaven,
To open them for Her!

W.H.Davies

Ghoul care

Sour friend, go home and tell the Pit
For once you met your master,
A man who carried in his soul
Three charms against disaster,
The Devil and disaster.

Away, away, and tell the tale
And start your whelps a-whining,
Say 'In the greenwood of his soul
A lizard's eye was shining,
A little eye kept shining.'

Away, away, and salve your sores,
And set your hags a–groaning,
Say, 'In the greenwood of his soul
A drowsy bee was droning,
A dreamy bee was droning.'

Prodigious Bat! Go start the walls
Of Hell with horror ringing,
Say, 'In the greenwood of his soul
There was a goldfinch singing.'
A pretty goldfinch singing.'

And then come back, come, if you please,
A fiercer ghoul and ghaster,
With all the glooms and smuts of Hell
Behind you, I'm your master!
You know I'm still your master.

Ralph Hodgson

Laugh and be merry

Laugh and be merry, remember, better the world
    with a song,
Better the world with a blow in the teeth of a
    wrong.
Laugh, for the time is brief, a thread the length of a
    span.
Laugh, and be proud to belong to the old proud
    pageant of man.

Laugh and be merry: remember, in olden time,
God made Heaven and Earth for joy He took in a
    rhyme,
Made them, and filled them full with the strong red
    wine of His mirth,
The splendid joy of the stars: the joy of the earth.

So we must laugh and drink from the deep blue cup
    of the sky,
Join the jubilant song of the great stars sweeping by,
Laugh, and battle, and work, and drink of the wine
    outpoured
In the dear green earth, the sign of the joy of the
    Lord.

Laugh and be merry together, like brothers akin,
Guesting awhile in the rooms of a beautiful inn,
Glad till the dancing stops, and the lilt of the music
    ends.
Laugh till the game is played; and be you merry, my
    friends.

John Masefield

Men who march away

We be the King's men, hale and hearty,
Marching to meet one Buonaparty;
If he won't sail, lest the wind should blow,
We shall have marched for nothing, O!
                    Right fol-lol!

We be the King's men, hale and hearty,
Marching to meet one Buonaparty;
If he be sea-sick, says 'No, no!'
We shall have marched for nothing, O!

> Right fol-lol!

We be the King's men, hale and hearty,
Marching to meet one Buonaparty;
Never mind, mates; we'll be merry, though
We may have marched for nothing, O!

> Right fol-lol!

Thomas Hardy

Napoleon

Children, when was
Napoleon Bonaparte born,
asks teacher.

A thousand years ago, the children say.
A hundred years ago, the children say.
Last year, the children say.
No one knows.

Children, what did
Napoleon Bonaparte do,
asks teacher.

Won a war, the children say.
Lost a war, the children say.
No one knows.

Our butcher had a dog
called Napoleon,
says František.
The butcher used to beat him and the dog died
of hunger
a year ago.

And all the children are now sorry
for Napoleon.

Miroslav Holub

The example

Here's an example from
    A Butterfly;
That on a rough, hard rock
    Happy can lie;
Friendless and all alone
On this unsweetened stone.

Now let my bed be hard,
    No care take I;
I'll make my joy like this
    Small Butterfly,
Whose happy heart has power
To make a stone a flower.

W.H.Davies

There was a young man

There was a young man of Quebec
Who was frozen in snow to his neck,
   When asked, 'Are you friz?'
   He replied, 'Yes, I is,
But we don't call this cold in Quebec.'

Anon.

The rescue

The wind is loud,
The wind is blowing,
The waves are big,
The waves are growing.
What's that? What's that?
A dog is crying,
It's in the sea,
A dog is crying.
His or hers
Or yours or mine?
A dog is crying.
A dog is crying.

Is no one there?
A boat is going,
The waves are big,
A man is rowing.
The waves are big,
The waves are growing.
Where's the dog?
It isn't crying.
His or hers
Or yours or mine?
Is it dying?
Is it dying?

The wind is loud,
The wind is blowing,
The waves are big,
The waves are growing.
Where's the boat?
It's upside down.
And where's the dog,
And must it drown?
His or hers
Or yours or mine?
O, must it drown?
O, must it drown?

Where's the man?
He's on the sand.
So tired and wet
He cannot stand.
And where's the dog?
It's in his hand,
He lays it down
Upon the sand.
His or hers
Or yours or mine?
The dog is mine,
The dog is mine!

So tired and wet
And still it lies,
I stroke its head,
It opens its eyes,
It wags its tail,
So tired and wet.
I call its name,
For it's my pet,
Not his or hers
Or yours, but mine –
And up it gets,
And up it gets!

Ian Serraillier

My dog Robbo

Mongrel dog Robbo up got,
Thumped 'is ol' tail
What's tied up loose like an undone granny
And wagger–wagged it quite a lot.

Mongrel body on four sticks
Mongrel napper full of tricks,
Mongrel pelt stuffed with tics,
Mongrel gob wet of licks.

Scraps out, sups all,
Nabs all eyes light on,
Scoffs tin tacks and half bricks,
Chews all teeth bite on.

Knocks the purr out of pussies,
Fights the legs on our bed,
Woofs the wind up red buses
And leaves them for dead.

Howl like a squeaky brake,
Stink like a bog,
You get under the world's skin
That's Robbo my dog.

Gareth Owen

Of the awefull battle of the Pekes and the Pollicles

Together with some Account of the Participation of the Pugs and the Poms, and the Intervention of the Great Rumpuscat

The Pekes and the Pollicles, everyone knows,
Are proud and implacable passionate foes;
It is always the same, wherever one goes.
And the Pugs and the Poms, although most people
    say
That they do not like fighting, yet once in a way,
They will now and again join in to the fray
And they
        Bark bark bark bark
        Bark bark BARK BARK
  Until you can hear them all over the Park.

Now on the occasion of which I shall speak
Almost nothing had happened for nearly a week
(And that's a long time for a Pol or a Peke).
The big Police Dog was away from his beat –
I don't know the reason, but most people think
He'd slipped into the Wellington Arms for a
    drink –
And no one at all was about on the street
When a Peke and a Pollicle happened to meet.

They did not advance, or exactly retreat,
But they glared at each other, and scraped their hind
    feet,
And started to
        Bark bark bark bark
        Bark bark BARK BARK
  Until you could hear them all over the Park.

Now the Peke, although people may say what they
    please,
Is no British Dog, but a Heathen Chinese.
And so all the Pekes when they heard the uproar,
Some came to the window, some came to the door;
There were surely a dozen, more likely a score.
And together they started to grumble and wheeze
In their huffery-snuffery Heathen Chinese.
But a terrible din is what Pollicles like,
For your Pollicle Dog is a dour Yorkshire tyke,
And his braw Scottish cousins are snappers and
    biters,
And every dog-jack of them notable fighters;
And so they stepped out, with their pipers in order,
Playing *When the Blue Bonnets Came Over the Border*.
Then the Pugs and the Poms held no longer aloof,
But some from the balcony, some from the roof,
Joined in
To the din
With a
        Bark bark bark bark
        Bark bark BARK BARK
  Until you could hear them all over the Park.

Now when these bold heroes together assembled,
The traffic all stopped, and the Underground
    trembled,
And some of the neighbours were so much afraid
That they started to ring up the Fire Brigade,
When suddenly, up from a small basement flat,
Why who should stalk out but the GREAT
    RUMPUSCAT.
His eyes were like fireballs fearfully blazing,
He gave a great yawn, and his jaws were amazing;
And when he looked out through the bars of the
    area,
You never saw anything fiercer or hairier.
And what with the glare of his eyes and his
    yawning,
The Pekes and the Pollicles quickly took warning.
He looked at the sky and he gave a great leap –
And they every last one of them scattered like sheep.

And when the Police Dog returned to his beat,
There wasn't a single one left in the street.

T.S. Eliot

Mr Smith

Mr Smith of Tallabung
Has very wicked ways,
He wanders off into the bush
And stays away for days.

He never says he's going;
We only know he's gone —
There's lots of cats like Mr Smith
Who like to walk alone.

He plays that he's a tiger,
And makes the dingoes run.
He scratches emus on the legs
And plays at football with their eggs,
But does it all in fun.

And then, one day, he's home again,
The skin all off his nose;
His ears all torn and tattered,
His face all bruised and battered,
And bindies in his toes.

He wanders round and finds a place
To sleep in the sun,
And dream of all the wicked things
That he has been and done.

Mr Smith of Tallabung
May be a bad cat;
But everybody likes him —
So that's just that.

D.H.Souter

There was an old lady

There was an old lady who said,
When she found a thief under her bed,
  'Get up from the floor;
   You're too close to the door,
And I fear you'll catch cold in the head.'

Anon.

Old lady

Her hair is grey and her face has wrinkles
She is as slow as a tortoise
Her wrinkles show more when she smiles at you.

She stands on her balcony
Bent down like an old tree
Waving to people passing by.

Geraldine Flatley (10)

The new duckling

'I want to be new,' said the duckling.
    'O, ho!' said the wise old owl,
While the guinea–hen cluttered off chuckling
    To tell all the rest of the fowl.

'I should like a more elegant figure,'
    That child of a duck went on.
'I should like to grow bigger and bigger,
    Until I could swallow a swan.

'*I won't* be the bond–slave of habit,
    I *won't* have those webs on my toes.
I want to run round like a rabbit,
    A rabbit as red as a rose.

I *don't* want to waddle like mother,
    Or quack like my silly old dad.
I want to be utterly other,
    And *frightfully* modern and mad.'

'Do you know,' said the turkey, 'you're quacking!
     There's a fox creeping up thro' the rye;
And, if you're not utterly lacking,
     You'll make for that duck-pond. Good-bye!'

But the duckling was perky as perky.
     'Take care of your stuffing!' he called.
(This was horribly rude to a turkey!)
     'But you aren't a real turkey,' he bawled.

'You're an Early-Victorian Sparrow!
     A fox is more fun than a sheep!
I shall show that *my* mind is not narrow
     And give him my feathers – to keep.'

Now the curious end of this fable,
  So far as the rest ascertained,
Though they searched from the barn to the stable,
  Was that *only his feathers remained*.

So he *wasn't* the bond-slave of habit,
  And he *didn't* have webs on his toes;
And *perhaps* he runs round like a rabbit,
  A rabbit as red as a rose.

Alfred Noyes

Modereen Rue

(i.e. the little Red Rogue – the fox)

Och, Modereen Rue, you little red rover,
By the glint of the moon you stole out of your
    cover,
And now there is never an egg to be got,
Nor a handsome fat chicken to put in the pot.
        Och, Modereen Rue!

With your nose to the earth and your ear on the
    listen,
You slunk through the stubble with frost-drops
    a-glisten,
With my lovely fat drake in your teeth as you went,
That your red roguish children should breakfast
    content.
        Och, Modereen Rue!

Och, Modereen Rue, hear the horn for a warning,
They are looking for red roguish foxes this
    morning;
But let them come my way, you little red rogue,
'Tis I will betray you to huntsman and dog.
        Och, Modereen Rue!

The little red rogue, he's the colour of bracken,
O'er mountains, o'er valleys, his pace will not
    slacken.
Tantara! tantara! he is off now, and, faith!
'Tis a race 'twixt the little red rogue and his death.
        Och, Modereen Rue!

Och, Modereen Rue, I've no cause to be grieving
For little red rogues with their tricks and their
    thieving.
The hounds they give tongue, and the quarry's in
    sight,
The hens on the roost may sleep easy to-night.
        Och, Modereen Rue!

But my blessing be on him. He made the hounds
    follow
Through the woods, through the dales, over hill,
    over hollow,
It was Modereen Rue led them fast, led them far,
From the glint of the morning till eve's silver star.
        Och, Modereen Rue!

And he saved his red brush for his own future
    wearing,
He slipped into a drain, and he left the hounds
    swearing.
Good luck, my fine fellow, and long may you show
Such a clean pair of heels to the hounds as they go.
        Och, Modereen Rue!

Katharine Tynan-Hinkson

Reynard the fox

And here, as he ran to the huntsman's yelling,
The fox first felt that the pace was telling;
His body and lungs seemed all grown old,
His legs less certain, his heart less bold,
The hound-noise nearer, the hill-slope steeper,
The thud in his blood of his body deeper.
His pride in his speed, his joy in the race,
Were withered away, for what use was pace?
He had run his best, and the hounds ran better,
Then the going worsened, the earth was wetter.
Then his brush drooped down till it sometimes
    dragged,
And his fur felt sick and his chest was tagged
With taggles of mud, and his pads seemed lead,
It was well for him he'd an earth ahead.

Down he went to the brook and over,
Out of the corn and into the clover,
Over the slope that the Wan Brook drains,
Past Battle Tump where they earthed the Danes,
Then up the hill that the Wan Dyke rings
Where the Sarsen Stones stand grand like kings.

At the second attempt he cleared the fence,
He turned half-right where the gorse was dense,
He was leading hounds by a furlong clear,
He was past his best, but his earth was near.
He ran up gorse to the spring of the ramp,
The steep green wall of the dead man's camp,
He sidled up it and scampered down
To the deep green ditch of the Dead Men's Town.

Within, as he reached that soft green turf,
The wind, blowing lonely, moaned like surf,
Desolate ramparts rose up steep
On either side, for the ghosts to keep.
He raced the trench, past the rabbit warren,
Close-grown with moss which the wind made
    barren;
He passed the spring where the rushes spread,
And there in the stones was his earth ahead.
One last short burst upon failing feet –
There life lay waiting, so sweet, so sweet,
Rest in a darkness, balm for aches.

The earth was stopped. It was barred with stakes.

John Masefield

Goodbat Nightman

God bless all the policemen
and fighters of crime,
May thieves go to jail
for a very long time.

They've had a hard day
helping clean up the town,
Now they hang from the mantelpiece
both upside down.

A glass of warm blood
and then straight up the stairs,
Batman and Robin
are saying their prayers.

They've locked all the doors
and they've put out the bat,
Put on their batjamas
(they like doing that)

They've filled their batwater bottles
made their batbeds,
with two springy battresses
for sleepy batheads.

They're closing red eyes
and they're counting black sheep,
Batman and Robin
are falling asleep.

Roger McGough

Car attack

On last year's Hallowe'en
A car hit Auntie Jean.
Unhinged by this attack,
My Auntie hit it back.

She hit it with her handbag
And knocked it with her knee.
She socked it with a sandbag
And thumped it with a tree.

On last year's Hallowe'en
A car hit Auntie Jean.
And now, my Auntie's better
But the car is with the wrecker.

Doug McLeod

The fair

The Fair is a fight: some are fighting for gain;
Some only for pleasure and some to cheat pain;
But that squinting old hag, with a voice like a knife
And tray of wire monkeys – she's fighting for life.

Eden Philpotts

My busconductor

My busconductor tells me
he only has one kidney
and that may soon go on strike
through overwork.
Each busticket
takes on now a different shape
and texture.
He holds a ninepenny single
as if it were a rose
and puts the shilling in his bag
as a child into a gasmeter.
His thin lips
have no quips
for fat factorygirls
and he ignores
the drunk who snores
and the oldman who talks to himself
and gets off at the wrong stop.
He goes gently to the bedroom
of the bus
to collect
and watch familiar shops and pubs passby
(perhaps for the last time?)
The sameold streets look different now
more distinct
as through new glasses.
And the sky
was it ever so blue?

And all the time
deepdown in the deserted busshelter of his mind
he thinks about his journey nearly done.
One day he'll clock on and never clock off
or clock off and never clock on.

Roger McGough

How they brought the good news from Ghent to Aix

I sprang to the stirrup, and Joris, and he;
I galloped, Dirck galloped, we galloped all three;
'Good speed!' cried the watch, as the gate-bolts
    undrew;
'Speed!' echoed the wall to us galloping through;
Behind shut the postern, the lights sank to rest,
And into the midnight we galloped abreast.

Not a word to each other; we kept the great pace
Neck by neck, stride by stride, never changing our
    place;
I turned in my saddle and made its girths tight,
Then shortened each stirrup, and set the pique right,
Rebuckled the cheek-strap, chained slacker the bit,
Nor galloped less steadily Roland a whit.

'Twas moonset at starting; but while we drew near
Lokeren, the cocks crew and twilight dawned clear;
At Boom, a great yellow star came out to see;
At Duffeld, 'twas morning as plain as could be;
And from Mecheln church-steeple we heard the
    half-chime,
So Joris broke silence with, 'Yet there is time!'

At Aerschot, up leaped of a sudden the sun,
And against him the cattle stood black every one,
To stare through the mist at us galloping past,
And I saw my stout galloper, Roland, at last,
With resolute shoulders each butting away
The haze, as some bluff river headland its spray;

And his low head and crest, just one sharp ear bent
    back
For my voice, and the other pricked out on his track;
And one eye's black intelligence, – ever that glance
O'er its white edge at me, his own master, askance!
And the thick heavy spume-flakes which aye and
    anon
His fierce lips shook upwards in galloping on.

By Hasselt, Dirck groaned; and cried Joris, 'Stay
    spur!
Your Roos galloped bravely, the fault's not in her,
We'll remember at Aix' – for one heard the quick
    wheeze
Of her chest, saw the stretched neck, and staggering
    knees,
And sunk tail, and horrible heave of the flank,
As down on her haunches she shuddered and sank.

So we were left galloping, Joris and I,
Past Loos and past Tongres, no cloud in the sky;
The broad sun above laughed a pitiless laugh,
'Neath our foot broke the brittle bright stubble like
    chaff;
Till over by Dalhem a dome-tower sprang white,
And 'Gallop,' cried Joris, 'for Aix is in sight!'

'How they'll greet us!' and all in a moment his roan
Rolled neck and croup over, lay dead as a stone;
And there was my Roland to bear the whole weight
Of the news which alone could save Aix from her
    fate,
With his nostrils like pits full of blood to the brim,
And with circles of red for his eye-sockets' rim.

Then I cast my loose buff-coat, each holster let fall,
Shook off both my jack-boots, let go belt and all,
Stood up in the stirrup, leaned, patted his ear,
Called my Roland his pet name, my horse without
    peer;
Clapped my hands, laughed and sang, any noise,
    bad or good,
Till at length into Aix Roland galloped and stood.

And all I remember is friends flocking round
As I sate with his head 'twixt my knees on the
    ground,
And no voice but was praising this Roland of mine,
As I poured down his throat our last measure of
    wine,
Which (the burgesses voted by common consent)
Was no more than his due who brought good news
    from Ghent.

Robert Browning

The Cavalier's escape

Trample! trample! went the roan,
   Trap! trap! went the grey;
But pad! pad! pad! like a thing that was mad,
   My chestnut broke away.
It was just five miles from Salisbury town,
   And but one hour to day.

Thud! thud! came on the heavy roan,
   Rap! rap! the mettled grey;
But my chestnut mare was of blood so rare,
   That she showed them all the way.
Spur on! spur on! I doffed my hat,
   And wished them all good–day.

They splashed through miry rut and pool,
   Splintered through fence and rail;
But chestnut Kate switched over the gate,
   I saw them droop and tail.
To Salisbury town, but a mile of down,
   Over this brook and rail.

Trap! trap! I heard their echoing hoofs
    Past the walls of mossy stone;
The roan flew on at a staggering pace,
    But blood is better than bone.
I patted old Kate and gave her the spur,
    For I knew it was all my own.

But trample! trample! came their steeds,
    And I saw their wolf's eyes burn;
I felt like a royal hart at bay,
    And I made me ready to turn.
I looked where highest grew the may,
    And deepest arched the fern.

I flew at the first knave's sallow throat;
    One blow, and he was down.
The second rogue fired twice, and missed;
    I sliced the villain's crown,
Clove through the rest, and flogged brave Kate,
    Fast, fast, to Salisbury town.

Pad! pad! they came on the level sward,
    Thud! thud! upon the sand;
With a gleam of swords, and a burning match,
    And a shaking of flag and hand.
But one long bound, and I passed the gate,
    Safe from the canting band.

G.W. Thornbury

The sailor's consolation

One night came on a hurricane,
    The sea was mountains rolling,
When Barney Buntline slewed his quid
    And said to Billy Bowline:
'A strong nor'-wester's blowing, Bill:
    Hark: don't ye hear it roar now?
Lord help 'em, how I pities them
    Unhappy folks on shore now.

'Foolhardy chaps as live in towns,
    What danger they are all in,
And now lie quaking in their beds.
    For fear the roof should fall in!
Poor creature, how they envies us
    And wishes, I've a notion,
For our good luck in such a storm
    To be upon the ocean!

'And as for them that's out all day
   On business from their houses,
And late at night returning home
   To cheer their babes and spouses;
While you and I, Bill, on the deck
   Are comfortably lying,
My eyes! what tiles and chimney-pots
   About their heads are flying!

'Both you and I have oft-times heard
   How men are killed and undone
By overturns from carriages,
   By thieves and fires, in London.
We know what risks these landsmen run,
   From noblemen to tailors;
Then, Bill, let us thank Providence
   That you and I are sailors.'

Charles Dibdin

Drake's drum

Drake he's in his hammock an' a thousand mile
      away,
   (Capten, art tha sleepin' there below?)
Slung atween the round shot in Nombre Dios Bay,
   An' dreamin' arl the time o' Plymouth Hoe.
Yarnder lumes the Island, yarnder lie the ships,
   Wi' sailor-lads a-dancin' heel-an'-toe,
An' the shore-lights flashin', an' the night-tide
      dashin',
   He sees et arl so plainly as he saw et long ago.

Drake he was a Devon man, an' ruled the Devon
   seas,
   (Capten, art tha sleepin' there below?)
Rovin' tho' his death fell, he went wi' heart at ease,
   An' dreamin' arl the time o' Plymouth Hoe.
'Take my drum to England, hang et by the shore,
   Strike et when your powder's runnin' low;
If the Dons sight Devon, I'll quit the port o'
   Heaven,
   An' drum them up the Channel as we drummed
   them long ago.'

Drake he's in his hammock till the great Armadas
   come,
   (Capten, art tha sleepin' there below?)
Slung atween the round shot, listenin' for the
   drum,
   An' dreamin' arl the time o' Plymouth Hoe.
Call him on the deep sea, call him up the Sound,
   Call him when ye sail to meet the foe;
Where the old trade's plyin' an' the old flag flyin'
   They shall find him ware an' wakin', as they
   found him long ago!

Henry Newbolt

The soldier

If I should die, think only this of me:
    That there's some corner of a foreign field
That is for ever England. There shall be
    In that rich earth a richer dust concealed;
A dust whom England bore, shaped, made aware,
    Gave, once, her flowers to love, her ways to
        roam,
A body of England's, breathing English air,
    Washed by the rivers, blest by suns of home.

And think, this heart, all evil shed away,
    A pulse in the eternal mind, no less
        Gives somewhere back the thoughts by
           England given;
Her sights and sounds; dreams happy as her day;
    And laughter, learnt of friends; and gentleness,
        In hearts at peace, under an English heaven.

Rupert Brooke

The charge of the Light Brigade

Half a league, half a league,
   Half a league onward,
All in the valley of Death
   Rode the six hundred.
'Forward, the Light Brigade!
Charge for the guns!' he said:
Into the valley of Death
   Rode the six hundred.

'Forward, the Light Brigade!'
Was there a man dismayed?
Not tho' the soldier knew
   Someone had blundered.
Theirs not to make reply,
Theirs not to reason why,
Theirs but to do and die:
Into the valley of Death
   Rode the six hundred.

Cannon to right of them,
Cannon to left of them,
Cannon in front of them
   Volley'd and thundered;
Stormed at with shot and shell,
Boldly they rode and well,
Into the jaws of Death,
Into the mouth of Hell
   Rode the six hundred.

Flashed all their sabres bare,
Flashed as they turned in air
Sabring the gunners there,
Charging an army, while
    All the world wondered:
Plunged in the battery–smoke
Right thro' the line they broke;
Cossack and Russian
Reeled from the sabre–stroke
    Shattered and sundered.
Then they rode back, but not,
    Not the six hundred.

Cannon to right of them,
Cannon to left of them,
Cannon behind them
    Volley'd and thundered;
Stormed at with shot and shell,
While horse and hero fell,
They that had fought so well
Came thro' the jaws of Death,
Back from the mouth of Hell,
All that was left of them,
    Left of six hundred.

When can their glory fade?
O the wild charge they made!
    All the world wondered.
Honour the charge they made!
Honour the Light Brigade,
    Noble six hundred!

Alfred, Lord Tennyson

Soldier Freddy

Soldier Freddy
  was never ready,
But Soldier Neddy,
  unlike Freddy
was always ready
  and steady,

That's why,
  When Soldier Neddy
Is–outside–Buckingham Palace–on–guard–in–the–
  pouring–wind–and–rain–
  being–steady–and ready
Freddy –
  is home in beddy.

Spike Milligan

The patriot

A ragged figure
Against the wall.
White shirt fluttering.
Watchers muttering.
So this is his fall!
Grey hills look down
On a fighter, a man
who loved his land.
The bells in the town
are quiet. Today they
cease their silver cry.
For the man who will die
men kneel in the church, and pray.
A good man was he – it was owned by all.
He'd drunk victory's wine.
He'd enjoyed it, was fine . . .
But now he must drink of the gall.
A fighter he'd been. Who could have held him?
But for the traitor that sold
him for miserable gold
he'd be in the hills yet,
in sunshine and wet,
the scourge of the Huns!
Who stole their guns?

Now a gaunt head is raised.
No tremor. Troops stare, amazed.
The rifles are levelled. 'Vive la France!' his last call.
Then a crack. Men weep.

That is all.

Graeme Iley (14)

Bruce's address before Bannockburn

Scots, wha hae wi' Wallace bled,
Scots, wham Bruce has aften led,
Welcome to your gory bed,
   Or to victorie.

Now's the day, and now's the hour,
See the front o' battle lour!
See approach proud Edward's power –
   Chains and slaverie!

Wha will be a traitor knave?
Wha will fill a coward's grave?
Wha sae base as be a slave?
   Let him turn and flee!

Wha for Scotland's King and law
Freedom's sword will strongly draw,
Freeman stand, or freeman fa'.
   Let him on wi' me!

By oppression's woes and pains!
By your sons in servile chains!
We will drain our dearest veins,
   But they shall be free!

Lay the proud usurpers low!
Tyrants fall in every foe!
Liberty's in every blow!
   Let us do or die!

Robert Burns

The feast of Crispian

This day is called the feast of Crispian:
He that outlives this day, and comes safe home,
Will stand a tip-toe when this day is named,
And rouse him at the name of Crispian.
He that shall live this day, and see old age,
Will yearly on the vigil feast his neighbours,
And say, 'Tomorrow is Saint Crispian:'
Then will he strip his sleeve and show his scars,
And say, 'These wounds I had on Crispin's day.'
Old men forget: yet all shall be forgot,
But he'll remember with advantages
What feats he did that day. Then shall our names,
Familiar in his mouth as household words,
Harry the king, Bedford and Exeter,
Warwick and Talbot, Salisbury and Gloucester,
Be in their flowing cups freshly remembered.
This story shall the good man teach his son;
And Crispin Crispian shall ne'er go by,
From this day to the ending of the world,
But we in it shall be remembered;
We few, we happy few, we band of brothers;
For he today that sheds his blood with me
Shall be my brother; be he ne'er so vile
This day shall gentle his condition:
And gentlemen in England now abed
Shall think themselves accursed they were not here,
And hold their manhoods cheap whiles any speaks
That fought with us upon Saint Crispin's day.

William Shakespeare

Love and glory

Young Henry was as brave a youth
   As ever graced a gallant story;
And Jane was fair as lovely truth,
   She sigh'd for Love, and he for Glory!

With her his faith he meant to plight,
   And told her many a gallant story;
Till war, their coming joys to blight,
   Call'd him away from Love to Glory!

Young Henry met the foe with pride;
   Jane followed, fought! ah, hapless story!
In man's attire, by Henry's side,
   She died for Love, and he for Glory.

Thomas Dibdin

Young Lochinvar

O, young Lochinvar is come out of the West!
Through all the wide Border his steed is the best;
And save his good broadsword he weapon had
    none;
He rode all unarm'd and he rode all alone.
So faithful in love, and so dauntless in war,
There never was knight like the young Lochinvar!

He stay'd not for brake and he stopt not for stone;
He swam the Eske river where ford there was none;
But ere he alighted at Netherby gate,
The bride had consented; the gallant came late;
For a laggard in love and a dastard in war,
Was to wed the fair Ellen of brave Lochinvar.

So bravely he enter'd the Netherby Hall,
Among bridesmen and kinsmen and brothers and
    all,
Thus spake the bride's father, his hand on his sword,
For the poor craven bridegroom said never a word,
'O come ye in peace here, or come ye in war,
Or to dance at our bridal, young Lord Lochinvar?'

'I long woo'd your daughter, my suit you denied;
Love swells like the Solway, but ebbs like its tide;
And now I am come with this lost love of mine
To lead but one measure, drink one cup of wine.
There are maidens in Scotland more lovely by far,
That would gladly be bride to the young
    Lochinvar!'

The bride kiss'd the goblet, the knight took it up,
He quaff'd off the wine and he threw down the cup;
She look'd down to blush, and she look'd up to
    sigh,
With a smile on her lips and a tear in her eye.
He took her soft hand ere her mother could bar;
'Now tread we a measure!' said young Lochinvar.

So stately his form, and so lovely her face,
That never a hall such a galliard did grace:
While her mother did fret and her father did fume,
And the bridegroom stood dangling his bonnet and
    plume;
And the bride-maidens whispered, ' 'Twere better
    by far
To have match'd our fair cousin with young
    Lochinvar!'

One touch to her hand and one word in her ear,
When they reach'd the hall door; and the charger
    stood near;
So light to the croupe the fair lady he swung,
So light to the saddle before her he sprung!
'She is won! we are gone, over bank, bush and
    scaur,
They'll have fleet steeds that follow!' cried young
    Lochinvar.

There was mounting 'mong Graemes of the
   Netherby clan;
Forsters, Fenwicks, and Musgraves, they rode and
   they ran;
There was racing and chasing on Cannobie lea;
But the lost bride of Netherby ne'er did they see.
So daring in love, and so dauntless in war,
Have ye e'er heard of gallant like young Lochinvar!

Walter Scott

The outlandish knight

An outlandish knight came from the North lands,
   And he came a wooing to me;
And he told me he'd take me unto the North lands,
   And there he would marry me.

'Come, fetch me some of your father's gold,
   And some of your mother's fee;
And two of the best nags out of the stable,
   Where they stand thirty and three.'

She fetched him some of her father's gold
   And some of her mother's fee;
And two of the best nags out of the stable,
   Where they stood thirty and three.

She mounted her on her milk-white steed,
   He on the dapple grey;
They rode till they came unto the sea-side,
   Three hours before it was day.

'Light off, light off thy milk-white steed,
    And deliver it unto me;
Six pretty maids have I drowned here,
    And thou the seventh shall be.

'Pull off, pull off thy silken gown,
    And deliver it unto me,
Methinks it looks too rich and too gay
    To rot in the salt sea.

'Pull off, pull off thy silken stays,
    And deliver them unto me!
Methinks they are too fine and gay
    To rot in the salt sea.'

'Pull off, pull off thy Holland smock,
    And deliver it unto me;
Methinks it looks too rich and gay
    To rot in the salt sea.'

'If I must pull off my Holland smock,
    Pray turn thy back unto me,
For it is not fitting that such a ruffian
    A woman unclad should see.'

He turned his back towards hers,
    And viewed the leaves so green;
She catch'd him round the middle so small,
    And tumbled him into the stream.

He dropped high, and he dropped low,
    Until he came to the tide –
'Catch hold of my hand, my pretty maiden,
    And I will make you my bride.'

'Lie there, lie there, you false-hearted man,
    Lie there instead of me;
Six pretty maidens have you drowned here,
    And the seventh has drowned thee.'

She mounted on her milk-white steed,
    And led the dapple grey.
She rode till she came to her father's hall,
    Three hours before it was day.

Anon.

Lament for Flodden

I've heard them lilting at our ewe-milking,
    Lasses are lonely and dowie and wae;
But now they are moaning on ilka green loaning:
    The flowers of the forest are a' wede away.

At bughts, in the morning, nae blythe lads are
        scorning,
    Lassies are lonely and dowie and wae;
Nae daffing, nae gabbing, but sighing and sabbing.
    Ilk ane lifts her leglin and hies her away.

In hairst, at the shearing, nae youths now are
        jeering,
    Bandsters are lyart, and runkled, and gray;
At fair or at preaching, nae wooing, nae fleeching:
    The flowers of the forest are a' wede away.

At e'en, in the gloaming, nae swankies are roaming
  'Bout stacks wi' the lasses at bogle to play;
But ilk ane sits eerie, lamenting her dearie:
  The flowers of the forest are a' wede away.

Dool and wae for the order sent our lads to the
    Border!
  The English, for ance, by guile wan the day;
The flowers of the forest, that fought aye the
    foremost,
  The prime of our land, lie cauld in the clay.

We'll hear nae mair lilting at our ewe-milking;
  Women and bairns are heartless and wae;
Sighing and moaning on ilka green loaning:
  The flowers of the forest are a' wede away.

Jane Elliot

The hero

'Jack fell as he'd have wished,' the Mother said,
And folded up the letter that she'd read.
'The Colonel writes so nicely.' Something broke
In the tired voice that quavered to a choke.
She half looked up. 'We mothers are so proud
Of our dead soldiers.' Then her face was bowed.

Quietly the Brother Officer went out.
He'd told the poor old dear some gallant lies
That she would nourish all her days, no doubt.
For while he coughed and mumbled, her weak eyes
Had shone with gentle triumph, brimmed with joy,
Because he'd been so brave, her glorious boy.

He thought how 'Jack', cold-footed, useless swine,
Had panicked down the trench that night the mine
Went up at Wicked Corner; how he'd tried
To get sent home, and how, at last, he died,
Blown to small bits. And no one seemed to care
Except that lonely woman with white hair.

Siegfried Sassoon

The Minstrel boy

The Minstrel boy to the war is gone,
In the ranks of death you'll find him;
His father's sword he has girded on,
And his wild harp slung behind him –
'Land of song!' said the warrior-bard,
'Though all the world betrays thee,
One sword, at least, thy rights shall guard
One faithful harp shall praise thee!'

The Minstrel fell! But the foeman's chain
Could not bring his proud soul under;
The harp he loved ne'er spoke again,
For he tore its cords asunder;
And said 'No chains shall sully thee,
Thou soul of love and bravery!
Thy songs were made for the brave and free,
They shall never sound in slavery!'

Thomas Moore

The Golden Vanity

A ship called *The Golden Vanity*
Saw a Turkish man–of–war at sea.

The ship–boy spoke. 'Captain,' said he,
'If I sink her, what will you give to me?'

The captain replied, 'You're brave and bold,
I'll give you a box of silver and gold.'

'Then tie me tight in a black bull's skin,
And throw me in the sea, to sink or swim!'

They tied him tight in a black bull's skin
And threw him in the sea, to sink or swim.

The water was cold, but he kept afloat,
And away he swam to the Turkish boat.

Some were playing cards and some throwing dice,
When he made three holes in the boat with his knife.

He made three more . . . Then – lose or win –
What did it matter when the sea rushed in?

Some cut their coats, some cut their caps
To try to stop the salt water gaps.

About and about and about swam he,
And back to *The Golden Vanity*.

'Now throw me a rope and pull me on board!
Captain, see that you keep your word!'

'I'll throw you no rope,' the captain cried.
'Goodbye. I leave you to drift with the tide.'

Out spoke the ship-boy, out spoke he,
'What if I sink you? How would that be?'

'Throw him a rope!' the sailors cried.
They threw him a rope – but on deck he died.

Anon.

Arithmetic

I'm 11. And I don't really know
my Two Times Table. Teacher says it's disgraceful
But even if I had the time, I feel too tired.
Ron's 5, Samantha's 3, Carole's 18 months,
and then there's Baby. I do what's required.

Mum's working. Dad's away. And so
I dress them, give them breakfast. Mrs Russell
moves in, and I take Ron to school.
Miss Eames calls me an old-fashioned word: Dunce.
Doreen Maloney says I'm a fool.

After tea, to the Rec. Pram-pushing's slow
but on fine days it's a good place, full
of larky boys. When 6 shows on the clock
I put the kids to bed. I'm free for once.
At about 7 – Mum's key in the lock.

Gavin Ewart

1805

At Viscount Nelson's lavish funeral,
    While the mob milled and yelled about the Abbey
A General chatted with an Admiral:

'One of your Colleagues, Sir, remarked today
    That Nelson's exit, though to be lamented,
Falls not inopportunely, in its way.'

'He was a thorn in our flesh,' came the reply,
    'The most bird-witted, unaccountable,
Odd little runt that ever I did spy.

'One arm, one peeper, vain as Pretty Poll,
    A meddler, too, in foreign politics
And gave his heart in pawn to a plain moll.

'He would dare lecture us Sea Lords, and then
    Would treat his ratings as though men of honour
And play at leap-frog with his midshipmen!

'We tried to box him down, but up he popped,
    And when he'd banged Napoleon at the Nile
Became too much the hero to be dropped.

'You've heard that Copenhagen "blind eye" story?
    We'd tied him to Nurse Parker's apron-strings
By G—d, he snipped them through and snatched the
        glory!'

'Yet,' cried the General, 'six-and-twenty sail
    Captured or sunk by him off Trafalgar –
That writes a handsome finis to the tale.'

'Handsome enough. The seas are England's now.
    That fellow's foibles need no longer plague us.
He died most creditably, I'll allow.'

'And, Sir, the secret of his victories?'
    'By his unServicelike, familiar ways, Sir,
He made the whole Fleet love him, damn his eyes!'

Robert Graves

Harp song of the Dane women

What is a woman that you forsake her,
And the hearth-fire and the home-acre,
To go with the old grey Widow-maker?

She has no house to lay a guest in—
But one chill bed for all to rest in,
That the pale suns and the stray bergs nest in.

She has no strong white arms to fold you,
But the ten-times-fingering weed to hold you—
Out on the rocks where the tide has rolled you.

Yet, when the signs of summer thicken,
And the ice breaks, and the birch-buds quicken,
Yearly you turn from our sides, and sicken—

Sicken again for the shouts and the slaughters.
You steal away to the lapping waters,
And look for your ship in her winter-quarters.

You forget our mirth,and talk at the tables,
The kine in the shed and the horse in the stables—
To pitch her sides and go over her cables.

Then you drive out where the storm-clouds
    swallow,
And the sound of your oar-blades, falling hollow,
Is all we have left through the months to follow.

Ah, what is Woman that you forsake her,
And the hearth-fire and the home-acre,
To go with the old grey Widow-maker?

Rudyard Kipling

No ordinary Sunday

No ordinary Sunday. First the light
Falling dead through dormitory windows blind
With fog; and then, at breakfast, every plate
Stained with the small, red cotton flower; and no
Sixpence for pocket-money. Greatcoats, lined
By the right, marched from their pegs, with slow
Poppy fires smouldering in one lapel
To light us throught the fallen cloud. Behind
That handkerchief sobbed the quick Sunday bell.

A granite cross, the school field underfoot,
Inaudible prayers, hymn-sheets that stirred
Too loudly in the hand. When hymns ran out,
Silence, like silt, lay round so wide and deep
It seemed that winter held its breath. We heard
Only the river talking in its sleep:
Until the bugler flexed his lips, and sound
Cutting the fog cleanly like a bird,
Circled and sang out over the bandaged ground.

Then, low-voiced, the headmaster called the roll
Of those who could not answer; every name
Suffixed with honour – 'double first', 'kept goal
For Cambridge' – and a death – in spitfires, tanks,
And ships torpedoed. At his call there came
Through the mist blond heroes in broad ranks
With rainbows struggling on their chests. Ahead
Of us, in strict step, as we idled home
Marched the formations of the towering dead.

November again, and the bugles blown
In a tropical Holy Trinity,
The heroes today stand further off, grown
Smaller but distinct. They flash no medals, keep
No ranks: through *Last Post* and *Reveille*
Their chins loll on their chests, like birds asleep.
Only when the long, last note ascends
Upon the wings of kites, some two or three
Look up: and have the faces of my friends.

Jon Stallworthy

What a life!

What a life!
My back stiff,
birds doing their droppings on me
in the middle of
Trafalgar Square.
Taller than anyone else,
I can't move an inch;
I can only see the people in front of me.
Snap goes light in front of my eyes.
I don't get washed often enough,
people stare at me as if they've
never seen me before.
I can't stick my tongue out—
it's too stiff.
I wish I could.
Noise noise noise
all I hear.
I feel empty.
Lord Nelson is my name and I
grow stiffer every day.

Raymond Barnett (9)

The Falkland hero

Sunburst sky filtering through to my hazy mind
As I leave the extended iceberg miles behind
A desolate barren island, one of nature's misfits
Then why do we fight, why do we have to die for it
And back home my wife and kids are dieted on
  anxiety
Ministers sleep tight on morals and we're blown to
  bits
The gold disc, petrified, submerges behind a
  shapeless cloud
Better encase my thoughts secure from harm's evil
  grasp
Shattering my tranquillity introduced by a hideous
  screech
Enters this chameleon in deceitful human form.
Way down below the grey troubled sea struggles on
There, amidst the turmoil, two minnows fight out a
  non-argument,
Whilst a whale acknowledges with his grotesquely
  sardonic smile
Odious blood erupts distorting my eyes draining
  my being
Cascading plummeting encapsulated in my metal
  tomb
'Scuse me sarge if I scream before I die.

Stuart Evans

At Greenham Common

During 1982 demonstrations to prevent long range
nuclear missiles being installed at US bases in
Britain were increasing. The women's peace camp
at the main gate of Greenham Common had
survived many official attempts to remove it. On
December 12 about 20,000 women came from all
over Britain and from Europe to link arms around
the perimeter fence. They decorated the wire with
baby clothes, toys, poems, pictures, woven
symbols and posters on the themes of love and
peace, as opposed to war and destruction; they
wove webs of wool on to the surrounding trees and
planted bulbs and seeds beneath them. Some stayed
all night, lighting fires and candles and camping in
the woods. The next day hundreds took turns to lie
down in the road and prevent access to the camp.

Inside this wire they want to bury bombs.
The concrete ramps lead gently to the sky
from secret savage underworlds
invested with annihilating power.
Here the silken silver fish can wait
to be let slip into another element,

releasing from one thought, or accident,
unprecedented average agony.
Whose longest night of doubt can lead us
from that end when fear is uppermost,
no quick death feasible? Two girls plant flowers
knowing love can work. Four armed guards watch
   them.

Aligned like prayer mats the ramps point east.
(They say the journey only takes six minutes.)
Before the monsters land, another shoal
will learn to fly, could reach the upper air
and pass them, heading west.
Not much survives such landings.

Ten thousand women linking hands around
nine miles of fence they decked with baby clothes
are chanting all together, 'Peace and freedom!'–
both of which they have, as yet, a portion.
In other places days like this can end
alone in gaol, expecting torture.

In Britain it has tempered argument.
For some have stayed to face derision
and the loss of lovers, or their children;
a few have been made ill or sent to prison;
all have learnt to live with mud and cold
and worried winter nights outdoors are long.

A young policeman, shivering in the rain,
was wondering if his mother would have come;
or if his grandfather had thought
that dying in the mud was brave or foolish;
what the next ten years might bring for him;
which children's toys to rescue from the wire

when, all at once, the women started screaming;
'Take those toys away from those boys!'

Jane Whittle

The dying airman

A handsome young airman lay dying,
And as on the aerodrome he lay,
To the mechanics who round him came sighing,
These last dying words he did say:

'Take the cylinders out of my kidneys,
Take the connecting-rod out of my brains,
Take the cam-shaft from out of my backbone,
And assemble the engine again.'

Anon.

The bombers

Whenever I see them ride on high
Gleaming and proud in the morning sky
Or lying awake in bed at night
I hear them pass on their outward flight
I feel the mass of metal and guns
Delicate instruments, deadweight tons
Awkward, slow, bomb racks full
Straining away from the downward pull
Straining away from home and base
And I try to see the pilot's face.
I imagine a boy who's just left school
On whose quick-learnt skill and courage cool
Depend the lives of the men in his crew
And success of the job they have to do.
And something happens to me inside
That is deeper than grief, greater than pride
And though there is nothing I can say
I always look up as they go their way
And care and pray for every one,
And steel my heart to say,
    'Thy will be done'.

Sarah Churchill

Ballad of the breadman

Mary stood in the kitchen
   Baking a loaf of bread.
An angel flew in through the window.
   'We've got a job for you,' he said.

'God in his big gold heaven,
   Sitting in his big blue chair,
Wanted a mother for his little son.
   Suddenly saw you there.'

Mary shook and trembled,
   'It isn't true what you say.'
'Don't say that,' said the angel.
   'The baby's on its way.'

Joseph was in the workshop
   Planing a piece of wood.
'The old man's past it,' the neighbours said.
   'The girl's been up to no good.'

'And who was that elegant fellow,'
   They said, 'in the shiny gear?'
The things they said about Gabriel
   Were hardly fit to hear.

Mary never answered,
   Mary never replied.
She kept the information,
   Like the baby, safe inside.

It was election winter.
　　They went to vote in town.
When Mary found her time had come
　　The hotels let her down.

The baby was born in an annexe
　　Next to the local pub.
At midnight, a delegation
　　Turned up from the Farmers' Club.

They talked about an explosion
　　That made a hole in the sky,
Said they'd been sent to the Lamb & Flag
　　To see God come down from on high.

A few days later a bishop
　　And a five-star general were seen
With the head of an African country
　　In a bullet-proof limousine.

'We've come,' they said, 'with tokens
　　For the little boy to choose.'
Told the tale about war and peace
　　In the television news.

After them came the soldiers
　　With rifle and bomb and gun.
Looking for enemies of the state.
　　The family had packed and gone.

When they got back to the village
　　The neighbours said, to a man,
'That boy will never be one of us,
　　Though he does what he blessed well can.'

He went round to all the people
  A paper crown on his head.
Here is some bread from my father.
  Take, eat, he said.

Nobody seemed very hungry.
  Nobody seemed to care.
Nobody saw the god in himself
  Quietly standing there.

He finished up in the papers.
  He came to a very bad end.
He was charged with bringing the living to life.
  No man was that prisoner's friend.

There's only one kind of punishment
  To fit that kind of a crime.
They rigged a trial and shot him dead.
  They were only just in time.

They lifted the young man by the leg,
  They lifted him by the arm,
They locked him in a cathedral
  In case he came to harm.

They stored him safe as water
  Under seven rocks.
One Sunday morning he burst out
  Like a jack-in-the-box.

Through the town he went walking.
  He showed them the holes in his head.
Now do you want any loaves? he cried.
  'Not today,' they said.

Charles Causley

Index of titles

Index of authors

More Beaver Books

On the following pages you will find some other exciting Beaver Books to look out for in your local bookshop

MARY HAD A CROCODILE AND OTHER FUNNY ANIMAL VERSE

Jennifer Curry

Inside these pages you'll meet all kinds of animals. There's a slinking lynx and rats with felt hats. You'll discover why the crocodile had toothache and what happened when a giant gorilla came to tea. And just in case you should chance upon a Horny-Goloch or Cyril the Centipede, you'll know exactly what to say . . .

CADBURY'S THIRD BOOK OF CHILDREN'S POETRY

Here is a fascinating collection of new poetry by young people. It is selected from the Cadbury's 1985 Poetry Competition which is part of the Cadbury's National Exhibition of Children's Art.

The result is a fresh and exciting selection of poems on a wide variety of subjects.

'Happy, sad, moving and very perceptive, covering myriad subjects' *Option*